From There to Here

by

William R. Lamb

Cover and interior images courtesy William R. Lamb.

www.innovativeinkpublishing.com
Send all inquiries to:
4050 Westmark Drive
Dubuque, IA 52004-1840

From There to Here

Lessons from the Saddle

Table of Contents

The Foreword

Ever heard the phrase, "Life is a Journey"? That's a silly question that would warrant a response of "only a thousand times." A better question would be, "Understanding that life is a journey, have you ever taken the time to reflect upon the part of that journey you've completed?" I mean have you ever sat down and revisited all the different people you have been and tried to understand how those people became the person you are today? Of course not. There's no time; you're in the middle of a journey. Unfortunately, (or fortunately, depending on how you look at it), journeys have an end. As we get older, that end becomes more apparent, and the value of our journey becomes increasingly more important.

I remember the day that it hit me like a ton of bricks. I realized that somehow a vast amount of time had passed, and I had no idea how. Let's see, I remember being a toddler, but barley. I more vividly remember those crazy teenage years. And oh yeah, I remember getting married and having children and starting a career. What took me less than a minute to recollect took me 59 years to live. Surely there should be enough to write a library of books, but there wasn't. There was just a short highlight reel. How had I allowed this to happen, and why the hurry to reach the end? Those are questions I wish I would have asked many years ago. I guess the good thing about the journey is that I'm still on it; there's still time to enjoy what's left of it. You are probably wondering what this has to do with a bicycle, and that's a good question, especially since I've only been riding a bike for the last five years. Well, the answer is quite simple. I was sitting on the saddle of a bike when I came face to face with myself, or at least the person I was forty years earlier. That one moment changed me forever, and for that I am forever thankful.

This book is simply one man's account of how easy it is to get lost during a journey and never really know that you are lost. I have learned many valuable lessons while on the saddle of a bike, and these are just a few. When you're lost it sometimes seems like a long road home, but in my case, it was only a bike ride away.

Chapter 1

Childhood

Childhood: the time in your life spent as a child under the care and supervision of others. A worry-free time filled with endless days of laughter and play. Days where you learn something new every five minutes, where naps are viewed as unnecessary interruptions, and you are kissed and hugged much more than you want to be. Sounds like a fairy tale, and to all too many kids in this world, it is. No part of that definition describes my childhood. Rarely have I ever given my childhood much thought, mostly because, in terms of the above definition, I never had one. What I had was an existence; in other words, I existed in the time frame most would describe as childhood. The thing is, I don't look back with anger or place blame on those who caused me to be there. I have always, for whatever reason, known that I have no control over past events and have thus never felt a need to waste time pondering them. The future was all that ever interested me, and I couldn't wait to get there. My siblings—I have 4 plus 5 step-siblings, and a few I'm not sure where exactly they fit in—in my opinion spent way too much time dwelling there.

The way I look at it, Dad and Mom were kids having kids, and they had no business doing so. We are all products of our environment, and they were no different. My dad had to quit school in the eighth grade to raise his siblings after he got them out of an orphanage, and my mom was one of four sisters—and that's all I know of her. Somehow, they married young and had five children in a row. Sue Francis was born September 13, 1956; Dorothy Louise was born May 15, 1958; William Ray Jr (that's me) was born July 6, 1959; Debbie Jean was born August 12, 1960; and Linda Ann was born July 28, 1961. What they were thinking, well, I for one have no clue, but that doesn't seem like a successful recipe for two uneducated and unsupervised young adults. I have little knowledge of their lives and have spent very little of my life with either of them—and even less with them together. I know they married and divorced each other several times, had other relationships along the way, and for the most part struggled as a couple. I have never questioned either parent on what took place when I was a child or why. I always thought they would have shared it if they wanted me to know. Even if they would have shared it, I'm sure the stories would be much different, thus serving no purpose. All I can say is that I love my mom and dad because they accepted God's gift and allowed me to be born. Dad and I now have a good relationship and talk frequently. Mom and I have seen each other very little in this life but promise to do better in the next.

I did a poor job as a parent, and I had many more resources than my parents did. It would be easy to blame my upbringing (as so many do) as to why I wasn't a good dad, but the truth is we must all accept responsibility for our own actions. I made the choices I made, and I knew (as do most of us) that many of them were not right and made them anyway. Accepting responsibility for one's actions is probably the hardest thing to do in life and the one thing that each of us puts off until the very end. So, in short, I love my mom and dad, and I forgive them for whatever they feel they need to be forgiven for when it comes to me. I hope they realize what a blessed life I've had and that they both hold a special place in my heart. I hope my sons someday feel the same way about me. We all fall short of what others expect from us, and no matter how hard we try we will never be perfect. My true Father always knew that and forgave me as He does all that choose to be forgiven. He is Lord.

Chapter 2

Remembering When I Met Me

I guess you could say the first time I remember me being me I was probably about the age of my grandson, four. What I'm saying is this is as far back as I can vividly remember. I was living with a very elderly lady named Emma Caroline Cook. She was my great-grandmother. She and I shared a one-room apartment that was built onto the edge of my grandmother's house. Our entire living space was maybe fifteen feet by fifteen feet, an estimation based on the knowledge I have today. It had a couch that folded into a bed, a sink on the wall, a small toilet in the corner with a curtain around it, a small refrigerator, and a stove. Our clothes were kept in a closet just outside the screen door that was on the porch we shared with the house. Inside the other part of the house lived my grandmother, Eva Perry, and a couple of her daughters. On the same property, just down the field a stretch, was an old rundown house my Uncle Robert lived in, and across the street was a small, well-kept little three-room house where Miss Birdy lived. She had a garden that she spent much of the day caring for. Our houses were separated by a red dirt road, and just behind us lived a colored family that raised hogs. In those days we were all referred to as coloreds or whites, I never questioned the language because as kids we were just kids living poor and enjoying the daily life on the red dirt road. I remember they would butcher those hogs and give us some of the meat occasionally. I'll never forget the first time I saw a hog hanging by its feet in the tree and its throat being cut—pretty scary when you're four years old. It may be crazy, but some of my earliest memories are political ones. We had a picture hanging above the table of John F. Kennedy that had his famous saying, "Ask not what your country can do for you, but ask what you can do for your country," so I guess the time I remember being me was about 1963. I didn't have much to do in those days; it was just me and who I thought was mom. Occasionally, a gentleman named Dr. Turner who carried a black bag would come by and visit. He would check me out by placing a thermometer in my mouth while listening to my heart and smiling. He would talk to great-grandma, and then he would leave. Another gentleman came by and held me up in front of what now I know was a car and kept telling me to look at this new blackbird. It turned out he was my dad, but I didn't know him at all. I had seen him there before, yelling and cursing and being drug off by the police, and at the time I remember thinking it was all so odd. For the most part life was simple, walking down the dirt road, looking in creeks, talking to Miss Birdy, listening to Uncle Robert shooting his shotgun off the back porch, and feeling the warmth of the sun. I'll never forget the rainy days on that red dirt road—they were great—or the mosquito truck as it filled the air with white smoke that I so eagerly played in, or the smell of trash burning as the night creped slowly in. I remember long summer days playing outside by the swing, looking at the sky, and while swinging once I thought I saw Jesus looking over a cloud looking down at me. That memory and vision I see as clearly today as I did then. That was probably the calmest time in my life. The crazy thing is, it seemed as though I was all alone in the world, and I felt it even at that age. I didn't feel like I belonged to anyone. I had no people and no deep feelings for anyone other than great-grandma. At least that's how I remember it.

Chapter 3

Meeting Mom, Dad, and Family

"What started out as just another day on the red dirt road ended as anything but. Those two people that I'd seen visit the green house on occasion and who screamed at each other a lot were back. This time they were there to see my great-grandmother. Their voices were raised for most of the conversation, and my great-grandmother was crying. The woman grabbed me and started away from the house. I could sense something was so wrong and immediately remember wanting my great-grandma to come and get me. We were going somewhere, but she wasn't coming. As we drove off, I remember that feeling of being alone again—only this time I was scared. The man and woman took me along with four little girls to a place in Dallas, Texas. I guess I was about 7 when I meet Mom and Dad. To the best of my knowledge, that may have been the first time I met my Uncle Ray and Aunt Connie, two people who later would play a huge role in my life. I remember crying a lot and asking for my great-grandma, who for me was still my mom, and then she showed up. "Please, let's go home," was all I could say, but instead she told me we were going to stay there together. I wanted to go back to the red dirt road and the mosquito truck, my swing, and the Florida rain, but that was not going to happen. I'm not sure of the events that occurred, but I remember while we lay in bed together one night great-grandma telling me she had to leave. I begged her to take me back to our home, and in tears she said, "They won't let me." "They can't stop me from going!" I said over and over as someone screamed from the other room to go to sleep and that I wasn't going anywhere. The next day she left me, and there was nothing I could do to stop it. I watched her leave, and I think a part of me left that wouldn't come back for quite some time. My great-grandmother passed away shortly thereafter. They took me to Florida to see her just before she died. At the time, she was somewhat mentally gone already and recognized no one around her. When I went to her bedside, she hugged me and said, "I miss you, little Ray." I don't remember feeling as sad as one would expect. After all, the woman I knew as Mom had done something no mom should do; she left me with people I didn't know. She left me, and I had done nothing wrong. She left me. The world I existed in at age eight seemed a bit like a fairy tale that I didn't like but couldn't keep those around me from reading it aloud. Alone in this world and being read a story I didn't care for, but deep down I knew someday I would control my own destiny. Many sleepless nights were spent dreaming of the day I would write a better fairy tale.

11

Chapter 4

From Pillar to Post

I guess we relocated back to Milton, Florida, because I remember being back at the green house on the dirt road when my grandmother Perry had an aneurism and passed away. My years between ages eight and fifteen were a blur to say the least. Mom and Dad must have been on the outs again because my sisters and I found a new home with my dad's mom, Lynn Johnson, a full-blooded Cherokee, and my step-grandad, Red Johnson. We lived in a little four-room house in the country with no running water or electricity. My Uncle Jimmy, Uncle Charlie, and Aunt Mary lived with us—that's right, eight of us shared a bedroom. We took baths in a washtub and shared the water, we shared clothes, shared a few toys, and shared many days playing in those woods. Many nights when I would have to use the restroom (or outhouse in our case), Grandma would make Charlie take me out there, and he would lock me in and scare me. I always got the last laugh because she would take a switch to him like there was no tomorrow. Red dug earthworms for a living, and being poor was all we knew. We had all we needed, I guess, because we got by. The feeling of being alone in the world was still with me, and I remember feeling as though that was okay.

I think at the time Mom and Dad were divorced again, but soon thereafter they must have reconciled because one day they drove up and took us with them. We rented a little house that backed up to Blackwater Bay there in Milton. Soon thereafter we wound up back in Texas. I remember that we stayed with Uncle Ray and Aunt Connie for a while but then back with Mom and Dad in an apartment somewhere. Dad was a mechanic, and one day he came home for lunch and almost ran over me while I was on a bike that he told me not to ride. That was my first close call on a bike but not my first time to be disciplined, to say the least. Getting lost on a Halloween night one street over was probably the worst bout I had with discipline, and that's enough of that story. Next, my sisters and I found ourselves back in Florida living in a small house just down from the airport and a block or so away from where my Grandma Johnson was now living with Aunt Mary and Uncle Jimmy. Red had passed away. At least this house had lights and water; it also had a room with a big box and a flag over it that my Uncle Billy was sent home in from Vietnam. My sisters and I fought like siblings do, but we got to know each other a bit better. We were growing up and had some history together, about two years of it. It was a challenge, to say the least, being a boy with four sisters. When something got broken, it was little Ray, and the vote was usually three to one. Sue, my oldest sister, was a bit more mature, in that her job for quite a while was to be a mom to the rest of us. I can only imagine what her book would be like to read. That place provided many memories, some good like a little girl named Charlene who lived around the corner and the sound of Hank Williams, George Jones, Loretta Lynn, and Conway Twitty on the stereo in the house every Sunday morning. Many memories in that house I'd like to forget but probably never will. Lots of drinking, physical fights, and us kids hiding under beds crying and scared to death or sneaking out windows running down to Grandma's to escape the violence. From there we moved to my grandfather's house, which was a really nice place. The surroundings, the house and the neighborhood, were better but the fighting just got worse. I came to realize Dad was an alcoholic and Mom was a bit of a flirt, and together they were a bad idea.

Since I had four sisters, I usually had to sleep on a couch by myself, and they shared a room. Many nights I lay awake asking God to please let me make it to an age where I could leave it all behind. I was probably ten years old by then. Dad and Mom soon did what they did best and left each other again. Mom and us kids moved to Sulphur Springs, and I'm not sure where Dad went. Mom was dating some guy named Slim, and if this sounds like fiction, I can assure you it's not. Days passed, and before I knew it Dad took me and a couple of my sisters away to live with him, which meant we soon found ourselves all together again—my sisters and I, that is—with Grandma Johnson. Dad was dating a lady named Fran, whom he soon married, and she became my stepmom. Fran had five kids of her own by a couple different husbands. There was Doug, Jeff, Kathy, Paula, Todd, and Ritchie. Fran had inherited some land, which she sold for $10,000, and she and Dad bought a gas station/restaurant with a small house behind it on Highway 82 in Paris, Texas. We lived there for a while before we moved to Colorado for a short stay. Uncle Charlie ran the place while we were gone, but we were back in no time, maybe six months. Dad and Fran fought worse than Mom and Dad, and we kids, well, we existed. Fran's kids all went to live with their dad, except Todd and Ritchie, both of whom my dad adopted. I guess I was about twelve at the time. That station somehow caught fire and burned, and we moved to a little house on Jefferson Road. I got a job at Amigos, a Mexican restaurant about a mile up the road, and had to walk back and forth to work. When I turned fourteen, I got my hardship license and bought my first car for $250. It was a 1967 four-door Dodge Polara with a 383 under the hood. I paid for that car by mowing yards and working at that restaurant. At that time in my life, I was paying for everything. I had to pay my insurance, buy my gas, make repairs to the car, buy my own clothes, and pay Dad and Fran a form of rent. Fran said it would make me learn responsibility. Life was tough living with Fran and Dad, but knowing what I know now, I'm glad it was. It taught me how to be self-sufficient and not have to depend on others. Times there were unfairly skewed, you might say, towards Fran's children. For example, I always had to mow because my stepsiblings were too young or had allergies, etc. When I would mow and be five minutes late for dinner, often the tea would be gone, and I would have to drink water because others had had seconds before I had firsts. Dad and Fran never really got along in those days—lots of fighting—which was something I'd grown accustomed to but was getting tired of. Seems I had been alone, as in watching out for myself, since I first became me. I was never shown any affection that I can remember from anyone. It's one of the reasons I guess that my grandson and I are so close. He knows beyond a shadow of a doubt that there is someone in this world who loves him beyond explanation, that will be there for him even after I'm gone. When we look in each other's eyes and smile, I know I've done right and left the world better than I found it. So I guess I owe that to those who raised me.

Chapter 5

Becoming a Man at Fifteen

L ittle did I know it, but that little house on Jefferson Road would play an important role in my life not once but twice, and some forty years apart. I remember going to school around the corner at Paris High school. In school I was a nobody really, and for me that was fine. I had played that role for some fourteen years. I ran track and was a pretty good pole vaulter on an all-black track team, more challenging than you might think. I worked hard at Amigos, did my chores at home, ran track, and was still able to maintain an A average in school. One of my friends asked me to go to a basketball game with him to watch his girlfriend play on my night off, and I did. I wasn't much of a basketball fan, but that night I became a fan of my friend's girlfriend. She gave me a note as they kissed goodbye with her number and the words "call me" on it. We started dating after she abruptly broke up with my friend Steve, and luckily, he was cool with it. I will never forget those days and especially those endless weekend nights with her sitting beside me in my '71 Cheyenne cruising Lamar between Sonic and Piggly Wiggly. For the first time, or at least in my eyes, I meant something to somebody. We laughed and learned a lot about love, or what we thought was love. My home life wasn't great, but I was gone as much as I could be, so all in all things were looking up. One night while she and I were out we spent a bit too much time gazing at the stars from the bed of my truck, and I arrived at that little house on Jefferson Road about fifteen minutes late of the time they had set for me to be home. My stepmom asked me where I had been, and I apologized for being late. She explained that it was their house and that they made the rules, and I was to follow those rules as long as I lived there. Again, I apologized, but again she began to lecture me. For some reason, I felt the need for the first time in my life to express myself. "Fran, I work hard, I do well in school, I do most everything that gets done around this place, and I pay rent. I am never late, and once again, I apologize."

"You do not talk to me that way. I am your mother." And then to my dad, she said, "Are you going to sit there and let him talk to me that way?" When she uttered those words my life forever changed. My dad said, "Ray, apologize to your mother," in his somewhat inebriated state. I replied, "I have three times, Dad, and she's not my mother." That probably wasn't the thing to say because at that moment those words meant that I was now a man at fifteen and would be treated as such. What happened between Dad and me is best left unsaid, but I ran out of that house to the security of my truck and said goodbye to existing in their world. Dad chased me but never caught me. I went to my sister Sue's house, and she took me in and protected me from Dad. Sue and her husband, George, didn't mind me living there for a while but soon decided I should go home, I guess. She was talking on the phone, and I was unaware that it was Dad she was talking to, at the same time she was telling me what Dad said he would do to me if I didn't go home. Unfortunately, (or fortunately—I guess it depends on how one views it), I let her know what I thought of Dad and Fran and the role they had played in my life thus far. Dad, hearing my remarks, was at the door to finish what he started before I knew it and again I made it to the safety of my car. I had traded my truck for a '68 Firebird 400 four-barrel convertible, and I used every cubic inch of that 400 to head as far away from that place as I could. I wound up staying with my friend, Brad McDowra, and his family for a while. At the time, Brad was dating a friend of my girlfriend's named Becky. I had a better job now at Sikes Grocery, and for once in my life I felt like I could breathe. I got a room at Camp Paris Motel, and that became my residence. It was tough to attend school as much as I was working and trying to pay all my bills. One day in English class with my favorite teacher, Ms. Winfrey, we were told to silently begin reading the next chapter, which I did. Several students in the class started goofing off, and before you know it she got pretty upset. "Take out a pencil and a piece of paper, and we will take a test on this chapter, and it will count on your six-week grade," she calmly said. I raised my hand and explained I hadn't finished the chapter, to which she replied, "Evidently, you all have by the actions you've displayed." Once again, I felt the need to express myself, and I said, "Ms. Winfrey, you know me. I've never caused you a bit of a problem. My grades are good. Why would you punish me for their acts? I can't pass this test, and I won't accept the grade." She looked as though she wanted to side with me, but for some reason said, "You will take the test and the grade." One never knows what's happening in someone's life, and I couldn't help but feel hers wasn't going great that day, but nonetheless I was tired. I was tired of a lot of things, and at that moment fighting the world become one of them. I picked up my books, took them to the office, and told the lady at the desk that I had better things to do with my time. And so went my high school experience. I was officially a man at fifteen, and quite frankly, I was ready to be what I wanted to be. No longer did I exist in someone else's world; now, I existed in mine.

Chapter 6

Footloose and Fancy-Free

Suddenly, I found myself in a world in which I had some control, and for the first time I felt free. One day while I was working at Sikes grocery my dad came in and demanded that I get my stuff and that we were returning to Florida. I respectfully declined, and Dad got pretty upset, but my manager, a young man himself, asked my dad to leave the premises or he would call the police. I can still hear Dad saying, "Have a nice life," to which I replied, "It's been a blast already." Knowing that I was finally out of the grasp of others and truly on my own was an answer to a prayer that I had prayed at least a thousand times.

Boy, did my life change in a hurry. Can you imagine being fifteen and living by yourself, great car, no curfew, no one to answer to, up when you please and out as late as you want? I was footloose and fancy-free. I had a couple good friends, Bobby Wright and Scott Ashmore, that I hung out with quite a bit. We learned to drink, play pool, partake of a little weed, and of course chase women. There are so many crazy things that happened in that period of my life that it would take forever to write them all down. Funny, now that I think of it, that was probably one of the happiest times of my life. I raced my car on Friday and Saturday nights at the Paris drag strip and spent most Sundays with Uncle Ray trying to help me put it back together. Uncle Ray and Aunt Connie lived on 4th Street, and you might say they served as my new parents on a regular basis. As I went through cars—and I did that a lot—Uncle Ray would cosign for me until my credit was established enough that I didn't need it anymore. They provided food and money when it was needed, and Aunt Connie provided prayer 24-7, as well as a lot of scolding in a language I never understood. She was Hispanic and extremely Catholic and one of the sweetest ladies I've ever met. My Uncle Ray is one of the most talented people I know. He is a great artist, author, and mentor, and he served as a father figure when I needed one most.

Aside from all the fun things one can do at that age with his girlfriend and friends, there were also crazy things that tend to happen. I got to know a police officer there (whose name I won't mention) quite well, or so I thought. He had stopped me one night and asked why I was out so late. I explained that I had nothing better to do, and he said he needed to follow me home and talk to my parents. "Pretty hard for me to do because I got to work tomorrow," was my reply, followed by, "Besides, I don't have enough gas to get there." After asking me to step out of the car, he placed me in the back of his and said, "Easy way or hard way—your choice." That definitely affected the tone of my voice, and I explained to him that my so-called parents lived in Florida and I at the Camp Paris Motel on the west side of town. He was reluctant to believe my story, but eventually, when I gave him my employer's name and my uncle's name and phone number, he began to believe me. He told me he could turn me in to truancy if he wanted and then lectured me on being out so late and not being supervised. He and I had a long talk that night about my life, and I thought we became friends because he graciously let me go. We talked from time to time and occasionally I would see him and squeal my tires to get his attention. He would always laugh and point his finger at me. Once, he asked me if I wanted to go ride with him, and of course I replied yes. After all, who doesn't want to hang with a cop after hours. He picked me up on a Friday night after his shift, and we rode the back roads of Detroit, Texas, a small town just outside Paris, in his Deuce and a quarter, Electra 225. He pulled out some weed, and we smoked a bit. I really didn't like the stuff, so I faked most of my turns. He got serious and opened his glove box and pulled out his pistol and then gave it to me. "That's pretty cool," I said and gave it back. Then he looked me in the eye, stopped smiling, and said, "You know I can't let you go, right?" At first, I didn't know if he was kidding or not. I begged him to put up the firearm and quit joking around. "You know I would never tell anyone about what we do," I said. He put the pistol to my head and sat there for what seemed like an hour but was more like one minute, and then he laughed and said, "You know I'm just playing, right?" After he put the gun up and we started driving back to town, I wanted to take that gun and shoot him. To say the least, I wasn't only scared—I was pissed. I made small talk until we got back to Paris, but when I got out of that car I told him what I thought about him in a not-so-printable way. I never saw him again, but a couple years later I thought I saw him in a parking lot in a squad car, so I went up to the car and said something to the effect of, "Where the hell you been, you piece of shit?" The next thing I know I was on the ground and handcuffed. I called him by his name and said, "What the hell is wrong with you?" to which he replied, "I'm not so and so. I'm his twin brother, and you never refer to an officer of the law the way you did." Quickly, I apologized and talked him into letting me go. To this day, I am not sure that wasn't him. Either way, I'd had enough of the cop thing.

Scott played in a band at the Texoma Club just across the OU/Texas line about 24 miles from Paris and the Orange Blossom in Paris, so lots of time was spent in those places drinking and shooting pool. You might ask how it's possible to drink at that age, but when you're with the band all is good. Donnie Watson, Archie Moore, and Scott Ashmore were pretty darn good and lots of fun to be around. Scott and I spent most of our time messing with girls while Bobby focused on pool. Crazy times indeed. My girlfriend and I had broken up for obvious reasons. Her parents thought I was a bad influence on her, and I probably was. During that time, Scott and I had several girlfriends who at some point were his and then at some point were mine. Maybe it was the kind of girls we were dating, or maybe it was the kind of guys we were—who knows? One night, my ex was with this rich kid in a nice charger a bit nicer than the Camaro I had but not by much. They rolled up beside me and broke a beer bottle on my car. He informed me to stay the hell away from his girlfriend. I did what any 16-year-old guy would've done; I turned my car into his and drove him into a parking lot, making both our cars not so nice. I got out and was about to take him out of the car when my ex grabbed my hand and said, "Let's go." Go figure. As it turns out, he was actually riding around with my girlfriend, his ex; he just didn't know it yet. We had a long talk before her sister met us to give her a ride home. The decisions I began to make got worse and worse. I offered to take one of my friend's wife and kids trick-or-treating since he had to work (he managed the local Sonic), and the next thing I know we were an item. One day she shows up with her car loaded, and we were living together. That lasted about two weeks. I kept Aunt Connie busy praying for me. My stepdad ran a big construction job in Forney, Texas, and my mom got me on there. I was making great money and moved into a brand-new apartment complex just outside of town. I had to spend a few weeks living in the Silver Spur Motel in Greenville until the apartments were ready. My ex and I were now convinced we were supposed to be together. I had made some strides with her family, as it appeared I was changing for the better, and all in all I was. A couple of unfortunate things happened that changed all that. One night, when I was going to pick her up, I was driving a bit fast and missed a curve that landed me about 30 yards out into a shallow creek. I had to walk down to her house and explain to her dad that someone ran me off the road. He used his tractor to pull me out. He smiled and said a guy would have to be doing darn near a hundred miles per hour to get a car that far out. He wasn't that smart; I was doing about 125. Our date that night consisted of a kiss and we will try again next weekend when I come back to town. I couldn't wait, the next weekend on my way there I decided to go through Sulphur Springs. While setting at a red light in my 1974 Red Firebird I got a bit too excited when the light turned and perhaps spun the tires a bit much. When I saw the carnival lights come on behind me, I pulled over and rolled the window down. I apologized to the officer who could have cared less and wrote me a ticket while being extremely rude. "You'll need to make arrangements to appear back here for court," he said. I said, "I'll just pay the ticket by mail," and he said, "No sir, you'll appear," and left the window. Now, my exact thought process was, "Well, then I guess I don't need this ticket," and I ripped it up, threw it out the window, and proceeded on my way. When the lights came on again, I simply didn't feel the need to hear any more of what he had to say, so I let the Firebird speak for me, and away we went. Soon the lights disappeared, and all was well again. After a bit, the lights appeared again; only this time it was a black and white, a state trooper, and like before we were off to the races. As I rolled into Paris, city cops in lime green cars were lined across the road, so I detoured behind the old KPLT radio station and to the backroads, and soon I was alone again. I made my way to a friend's house and parked my car in his backyard. His first words were, "Are you crazy? I've been listening to the police scanner, and you're the headliner tonight." I laughed it off and asked for his keys. He allowed me to use his car, and I picked up my girl and had a great night. At about 3 am I told him I was going to head back to Forney, that I felt it was the best chance to leave town without being seen. As I drove the empty streets I spotted a squad car so I made a turn by Wise park and pulled in and cut the lights. There was a tan Chevy pickup beside me, and it turned out to be a guy I went to school with whose dad was chief of police. He smiled and waved, so I didn't think anything of it. I sat there for a couple minutes, and then I saw a couple cars approaching from both ends of the street. They pulled in behind me and turned on the big lights. After asking me for my license and registration, I made a joking remark, "Sure, if I can see your gun." Quickest way for one's face to hit the ground, if one desires that, is to use that remark. I didn't make it back to Forney and lost my license for six months. They gave me a permit to drive to and from work only—all in all, not a good idea. Thanksgiving was coming up, so my girl and I had a great plan. We told her parents that we were going to hang out with my mom for Thanksgiving for a couple days, and they agreed. We spent a wonderful couple of days in my apartment in Forney, and no one would have ever known if it wasn't for Brad's girlfriend. Remember Brad, the guy I stayed with after sis kicked me out. Well, his girl and mine were friends and discussed that weekend on a phone call with my girl's mom on the kitchen phone unbeknownst to them. Our days together were done. One day I got a call from the friend whose house I parked behind, and he wanted to know if he and his girlfriend could stay with me a bit and if my stepdad could give him a job. I said, "Of course, but last time I checked you were married." He said they were through, and he also needed a ride. The weekend I went to pick them up I let a friend from work use my apartment for a small party with his friends. When we arrived back the place was full of half-dressed people with beer cans and alcohol everywhere, not to mention a fog of weed. I got everyone up and threw them out, gave my friend and his girl my bed, and crashed on the couch. Next morning, I went to work early, and about lunchtime a state trooper stopped and asked for me. He placed me in his car and took me back to my apartment where several police cars were. Once inside, I saw my friend on the couch beside his wife. The officer explained the girlfriend was fourteen and that I had transported her across county lines and could be charged for kidnapping. They took my friend and told me not to leave town and that drugs were found in the apartment. For once, I saw the severity of the situation and calmly explained how all this came to be. The officer said he believed me, but I wasn't to leave town. As soon as all were gone, I left town as quickly as I could and went to Uncle Ray's. I borrowed his old Ford truck, and Scott and I went and loaded all my stuff and headed back to Paris for good. We did have a little to drink along the way and put a small dent in Unc's truck, but it could easily be blamed on someone else. I got a job back in Paris and drove Uncle Ray's truck for a couple weeks since I didn't have a car to drive while my new car was being painted. I got rid of the firebird—it was bad luck—and was building a 1970 Roadrunner. The last six weeks had been terrible and couldn't get worse, I thought. I received a letter from my girl that the weekend may have created more of a problem than we thought—a child was in our future. I remember driving to her house to explain to her parents that we wanted to get married and make things right. Her dad was in the carport and said to me, "Son, you best leave, and I mean now." I tried to explain, but then mom came out with a small caliber pistol, and as dad was trying to get it away from her, I was trying to get away from there. I went straight to Unc's house to explain the problem and get help. I was terrified I would go to jail for statutory rape since she was underage and I was living as an adult. I remember thinking if I were married what could they do to me, a child thinking like a child. I passed Brad's girl that night, and she got in the car and said she heard what had happened. I told her that if I were married maybe they would leave me alone. I honestly don't know what I was thinking. I loved my girl, but I didn't want to be jailed and to live life again as I had for most of my life, with someone else controlling my fate. Brad's girl surprised me with, "Let's do it." "Excuse me?" I said. And she said, "Let's get married if it will help." Crazy as that sounds, we went to the courthouse, but I needed a signature since I was underage, so we drove to Florida and Dad signed for us. And just like that, I was where my parents had probably been, too young and married. Even though the plan was to be married for a short time until this blew over, one thing led to another, and we slept together. Fate is a cruel thing. I still have the letter that my girl sent saying her parents had agreed to us marrying. What I had done ended what I guess was never meant to be, and I wouldn't hear from her for many years. My wife and I had a son, and before I knew it, I was a dad. Although I didn't drink a lot, I was a horrible dad. My wife's family were the best people one could hope to have as in-laws. I wish I could have been the son-in-law they deserved. One thing was for sure—the footloose and fancy-free days were no more.

MY 1974 Pontiac Firebird

Chapter 7

My Big Break

With wives I've been extremely lucky twice. My first wife was a great person and still a friend to this day. I know she loved me, and she was much more committed to the relationship than I was. We were kind to each other, and we both loved our son. Looking back, the way I defined love then as opposed to now is quite different, and I feel I owe my first son a real apology. I worked at the highway department during the day, a gas station after work, and then sometimes loaded trucks at Campbell's Soup from midnight till 3 a.m. Having fun became playing softball with a team called the Hustlers. We all were good friends and had one of the better teams in that area. There was still something missing in my life, and I still felt as though I was alone. Uncle Ray got me a job with Genie, an automatic garage door opener company that he worked for. I began traveling and soon had my own territory. The money was good, and my eyes were opened to a whole new world. My clients treated me with respect, and I stayed at nice hotels and had nice meals. I drove a nice car, but after my first car all my cars were nice. I bought a brand-new 1977 Trans Am and was the talk of that small town. My wife and I drifted farther and farther apart for several reasons but being on the road a lot probably didn't help.

One day, in the summer of 1980, Bobby Wright decided to go with me on one of my trips to see customers in the Austin area. As we traveled through Waco I stopped and looked at a boat at Prikryl marine out by the airport and wound up buying it a short time later. I always loved boats for some reason. After seeing some clients on Thursday and Friday we decided to go out and play some pool. Bobby had asked around and was told of a place named Courtyard Blues, so we set out to find it. For some reason, we couldn't find it, but while looking we spotted a place where a ton of young people were going in and out, a place called the Silver Dollar. We looked at each other, and Bobby said, "Let's do it." We went in played a little pool and had a few drinks, and before you know it, Bobby was making money and I was drinking and cheering him on. After maybe having a bit too much, I told Bobby to pick the best-looking girl in the place and I'd take her home. He looked around a bit, pointed to a young lady, and said, "Her." Then he said, "You're married, dipshit. No matter, you have no chance," and he went back to his pool. Bobby was never short on letting you know how he felt. I thought about what he said. I was married but only by definition at the moment, and I really had no chance with this girl. A tall, beautiful blonde with big blue eyes and a beautiful smile. I'll never forget her white pants and black tub top, definitely out of my league. What the hell, I thought, and over I went. I said, "Would you like to dance?" She surprised me and said yes. We spent the rest of that night dancing under the silver ball in the middle of the dance floor. Actually, she was dancing, and I was trying not to step on her feet, with little success I might add. The movie *Urban Cowboy* had just come out, and the band played a lot of songs from that movie. One in particular, "Looking for Love," by Johnny Lee, later would become our song. No, I didn't take her home, but it wasn't because I didn't try. I did ask her to marry me and made it official with the ring off a beer can. I remember getting her number and being afraid it wasn't really her number but rather a false one just to be nice. I talked her into taking my ID bracelet, a definite reason to see each other again. Turns out, a mere four and a half months later, she and I were married and still are to this day.

After I returned home from the trip I told my wife about Cheryl and I left soon thereafter. That decision took a toll of me for quite some time. After Cheryl and I were married I would wake up in sweat from bad dreams often. The dreams were always about me being torn in two directions and no matter which way I turned, I always felt I made a mistake. In my dreams my son and my first wife would always beg me to stay and I would, then I would panic that I let Cheryl go and try so hard to get her back to no avail. Sometimes the dreams were in reverse and all in all I knew I would never be able to put away the hurt or pain I had caused all involved. Only recently have I laid it down. Becky, my ex-wife, married a good man shortly after and they have had a great life together. Cheryl and Becky are friends as are Becky and I which helps. We have more in common now than ever in the form of some beautiful grandchildren that we both love.

I'm not sure why God chooses to bless some more than others, but I know meeting Cheryl was the best thing that could have ever happened in my life. She came from an educated and well-respected family. Her dad was a superintendent of schools, and her mom was a piano teacher. My wife was graduating from Southwest Texas State and had just accepted her first teaching job. Her mother quickly became my mother, and her father my mentor. They took me in with all my faults and immediately began their quest to make me a better person. We had a simple wedding with her mom and grandmother doing all the decorations and making the cake. Her brother, Mark, was my best man. The whole thing, as simple as it was, seemed like a red-carpet affair coming from where I had come from, perhaps like a scene from a movie. Our wedding had its share of drama, as everything in my life seemed to have. My divorce became final the day before our wedding, my wife-to-be didn't know the divorce wasn't final until a few days before that. I thought that when you filed for divorce and signed the papers, you were done. When we decided to get married, I told her I was divorced, and I thought I was. Had we scheduled the wedding a day earlier, we would have had to postpone it. The night before the wedding her brother and I went out for my bachelor party, which was pretty much he and I having a few beers. That night we picked up a hitchhiker and gave him a ride. He sat in the back with my coat, which had my wallet in it. All the money for the honeymoon was in that wallet. Along the way, I realized the wallet was missing, and we both were sure the guy had taken it. I was distraught to say the least, but when I pulled up to the church to let Mark out at his car, there my wallet was lying in the parking lot. It would be a miracle if this wedding ever happened. Despite it all, the next day we were married. My wife's mom, Bonnie, made several people sit on my side because I had no family except my Uncle Ray and Aunt Connie. She was the most caring person I had ever met. Before we knew it, we had a son on the way—Nicholus Jason Lamb. My wife taught, and I worked at the highway department in a field party and soon became an inspector. I played softball for Schlitz Malt Liquor, a semi-pro team in Waco. Several things brought softball to an end starting with several injuries and finally ending with an incident that happened at four-thirty in the morning while heading to Dallas to play in a softball tournament. A friend of mine named Terry was driving, and my eight-months pregnant wife was asleep in the backseat. Terry took out a pistol, unloaded it, and gave it to me. He said this was the gun he'd like to trade for my derringer. I wasn't truly interested in trading, but I looked it over and said that I'd think about it. I took the bullets and placed one in the first chamber when Terry grabbed the gun and said, "Hold up, I want to show you the firing pin and what I'm going to have done to it." I somewhat listened while he was talking, but I was watching the road more than watching him because he was driving, and I am a horrible passenger. I heard the revolver spin and the hammer click once and shouted, "Wait!" At that moment, the pistol fired, and smoke filled the car. Cheryl sat straight up in the back seat and looked like she had seen a ghost. I asked if he was okay. "I think so," he said. "Where did you fire it?" I asked. He pointed downward. We turned the light on and saw that the bullet was plugged in the steering wheel just above his knee. Terry was a tall guy, and the Mazda we were in was small. The only other words said that morning were spoken by my wife: "Turn the car around and take me home…NOW." Thus, I retired from the sport. Cheryl's dad wanted better for us and talked me in to getting my GED and going to college. I started attending McLennan Community College. Mark had introduced me to golf, and I had fallen in love with the sport. One of Cheryl's mom's friends, Earl Patterson, was working at a small lighted par three course named Segos, and they had an abandoned trailer on the property they allowed us to live in for very little rent. I got a job at Curry Office Supply part-time and took a full load of courses every semester. The par three was run-down, the lights didn't work, and there were several junk cars scattered throughout, but it was great—and my golf game got much better. I had many wonderful times at that place playing with Earl, Ralph, Harvey, and others. Having a child with my wife working and me going to school full-time was tough, but we managed. I decided to try out for the McLennan golf team coached by Bob Ammon, another friend of Cheryl's family. I remember strolling up to tryouts with my Jack Nicklaus Golden Bear irons and woods under some sock covers and a brand-new Walmart bag and pull cart; I was clearly the favorite. I shot the best round of my life that day—and it was also the highest round of the tryouts. I think I shot eighty-three, and sixty-five made it. I asked Bob what I needed to work on, and in a nice way he said I had started golf too late and would never play collegiate golf, but I should continue to play and enjoy the sport. After finishing MCC, I enrolled at East Texas State, and my wife and I moved into married housing there. Neither of us had jobs, and we didn't make it there a semester, plus I wanted to play golf. My next blessing came in the form of a man, Mac Hickerson, the golf coach at University of Mary Hardin Baylor. He asked me to come try out, and I did. I didn't play well—shot 84—and will never forget his words. Instead of "I'm sorry," which is what I expected, he said, "Mary Hardin Baylor and myself would love for you to be a part of our family." I was stunned. He told me that his program needed bright young men, and he really felt strongly about me being a Crusader. If Cheryl had been the best decision I had made to date, accepting Coach Hickerson's offer was the second.

While I was attending Mary Hardin Baylor, things got kind of tight. It was difficult for me to drive forty miles one way to school and back every day. I was always taking at least seventeen hours to get through quicker. I had qualifying for golf in the afternoons, which left little time for work. I was also majoring in mathematics and minoring in biology, which made my course load extremely tough with lots of homework, *and* we had a child. What that basically meant was that we survived on Cheryl's salary. I did work part-time at Lake Waco Country Club as a bag room boy for Larry Salter, who was the head golf professional there. The owners were nice enough to let Cheryl and me live in an old house they had, just down the street from the club, for free. It was hard to classify that place as a house. It was more like a little square haydite block building split into four rooms, two were used as bedrooms, one as the kitchen, and one as the living room, and there was a little four-by-four-foot bath attached to the back. Before we moved in, Cheryl washed it out with a water hose. We fixed it up the best we could and survived knowing that when I graduated, it would get better. Some crazy things happened in that house. I remember Cheryl was getting ready for school one morning, and while standing in the little bathroom the ceiling was so rotten that it caved in and fell on her hair. She cried, and I felt horrible. I also remember at night knocking a scorpion off her face while we were lying in bed. My time at Mary Hardin Baylor with Coach Hickerson and my teammates are some of the best memories I have. I made some good friends there, and one of them, Joel Williamson, became probably the best friend I ever had. After I graduated from Mary Hardin Baylor, we were able to buy our first house, a brand-new brick home on Indian Springs Drive. I took a job coaching and teaching at China Spring High School, the school her dad had built from nothing and where he had served as superintendent for twenty-three years. He had retired, and Jimmy Carpenter, a good friend of mine and fellow golfer, had become the new superintendent. I taught algebra 2, calculus, pre-algebra, and consumer mathematics, and I drove a bus as well as coached the golf team. We had been sharing an old car that Cheryl had through college, a Toyota Corolla she had named Tosha, and we were finally at a place where we could retire her.

It's hard to believe how my life had changed. I went from being a high school dropout to a guy who played college golf and then graduated with a degree in mathematics, a minor in biology, and a teacher certification. From living in a small, run-down motel to living in a brand-new brick house. From driving a 1976 Toyota to driving a brand-new Pathfinder. I now had a family that loved me, a beautiful wife and son, a career, and, most of all, a purpose in life. My prayers had been answered; my storms were behind me.

Cheryl when we first met

Chapter 8

My Restless Soul (Following in the Path of My Inheritance)

This chapter was difficult for me to write, especially with where I am now in my life. Looking at my life before this, there were lots of bad things happening of which I had no control, but they were happening to me. This time I was the one to blame, and I hurt others who never deserved to be hurt. Hurt, in general, tends to be very messy, and once given it cannot be taken back. The giver is usually the one who carries it the longest. Most things in life begin to deteriorate if they are not attended to, and relationships are no different. You would think, knowing where I came from and considering where I was in life at that point, I would be quite content. I don't know, maybe it was just in my blood. Being restless could have simply been an inherited trait. On one hand, my life was good. I had a good job, a brand-new house, nice car, beautiful wife, and a ten-year-old boy. On the other hand, my life was somewhat boring. My wife and I were busy raising a child and working all the time to pay bills, and we simply drifted apart. I deserve the blame. After all, my wealth of knowledge when it came to relationships was that they lasted about six months, and we had far surpassed that. Seems I was still searching for something, but I had no idea what. Looking back, I guess at that point in my life I still needed to feel wanted. It's not that Cheryl didn't make me feel that way or that anyone could've; I was simply lost. Leaving out the unnecessary details, simply put, I made a mistake. I lived a lie for quite some time before it caught up with me, as lies tend to do with us all. I came home one afternoon, and my wife and my lie both confronted me at the same time, and what made matters worse was that both their mothers and my 10-year-old son were there as well. That went about how one would expect it would.

Ultimately, Cheryl and I separated. She moved to West, and I stayed at the house. I wasn't sure what to do or which way to go. The mistake I had made didn't feel like a mistake; it felt right, and I found myself in a position I could have never prepared for. At that time in my life, I had no idea what it meant to love someone or to be loved. The way I viewed love, I had now found it with two different people. To say I was lost would be an understatement. I had to move out of the house; I just couldn't afford it. I had resigned from my job and was working part-time at the Lake Country Club. Cheryl and I tried to reconcile, but we both struggled with the situation, mostly because I struggled with which way to go. I leased out my house and moved to an apartment at Baylor University and began my master's program, while Cheryl taught school in West and was raising our child. My life was now that of my parents, and I realized I was not yet free from my past. I was hurting a lot of people, and none of them deserved it. I was lost in a storm with no idea how to make it end. Sometimes we just need a reason to move forward, and mine came with the arrival of my youngest son, Trevor, the result of one of Cheryl's and my attempts to set things straight. At that time, a part of me was acting as though I was fifteen again and could do anything I wanted, while another part of me was dying inside knowing what I was doing was wrong. Cheryl was raising our kids, and I was doing as I pleased. Cheryl's mom came by several times to see me. She would say, "Ray, you are better than this, and my daughter loves you with all her heart. Don't make this mistake." She didn't treat me like I was just a son-in-law but like I was family, and with way more respect than I deserved. Not long after that, Cheryl's mom was diagnosed with cancer, and her dad and mom had just split up. It was a storm as bad as the ones I had been raised in, only I was part of the problem and no longer an innocent party. I spent quite a bit of time with Cheryl's dad, who was in a bad storm himself. What seemed like a storybook family was falling apart, and I couldn't help wondering if I was partly to blame. With what I am sure was a gentle shove from God, I did the right thing and reconciled with my wife. We moved back in our house and began to live as a family again. I could write a whole book about this chapter of my life, but it's one that I don't like to revisit. I saw enough hurt in my early life at the hands of others to last a lifetime, and now I had allowed myself to become the one hurting others. Looking back and seeing what I missed with my kids is a regret that I'll take to the grave. Wisdom, they say, comes with age, and age, well, it comes too fast. I'm not sure if Cheryl ever recovered from this time in her life. She had done everything the way she was raised to, she continued to serve the Lord, and her payment was a husband who let her down, a struggle raising kids on her own for a while, a mother who was a true saint dying of cancer while being separated from her husband, and a heart that was broken from it all. Her storm was just beginning, and I had helped create it. Being lost is a terrible thing, and I spent too much of my life there. Funny thing about storms is that it seems we always find ourselves going into or coming out of one. Another funny thing about storms is that they are never without reason, and it's often years before we understand the meaning of the rainbow that follows.

Chapter 9

Making Myself Somebody (Blue Skies and Only a Hint of Rain)

1992–2008

y wife and I reconciled, I graduated from Baylor University with a master's degree, and I went to work full-time at Lake Waco Country Club. Soon I became the assistant golf professional and really worked hard to change the image of the club. I begin to give a lot of golf lessons and soon developed a name for myself as an instructor. Larry encouraged me to enter the PGA program, and over the next couple years I earned my PGA professional status. There wasn't a lot of room for me to advance at the club; Larry had been the professional there since he was seventeen years old. I needed to be more. I needed to be somebody again, and not the guy who threw everything away. At some point, the little par three golf course where Cheryl and I had lived when I first went to school, was for sale. I decided I would buy it, make into a teaching facility, and start a good junior program. All my friends thought I had lost my mind. I was making more giving lessons than I was working behind the counter. Inside I knew I could make it work, and so I worked out a deal with Ms. Seago to buy the place if she would owner finance it. First, I sold the trailer and the old cars and cleaned the place up. There wasn't a driving range, but there was a large field that was part of the property, so I shredded it as low as I could with the old tractor that came with the place. I purchased a green hitting mat and had students hit balls into that field from the small parking lot. At night I had to go pick those balls up by hand with a flashlight so that I could use them the next day. I had plenty of incentive to help my students get better—the straighter they hit, the easier the balls were to find. Soon I raised enough money to build an eight-station covered hitting area with an office and a driving range with lights. Each hitting bay had a heater, so golfers could practice even when it was cold and raining. My hitting bay was equipped with a video system a friend of mine, Tim Cutshall, and I had put together. I could show a student their swing, draw on the screen, and even send them home with a VHS tape of the lesson complete with sound.

My junior program grew quickly and became my passion. What started as a Saturday morning clinic with five kids became an all-day affair with over a hundred kids. Several parents helped, and one, Ron Ewing, became a huge part of the program. He was as responsible as

I was for the early success. Another person who played a huge role was Old Charlie, at least that's what everybody called him. Charlie and I became friends at Bob Ammon's driving range. (Remember Bob Ammon, the MCC coach whose team I had tried to qualify for when I began my education?) Charlie was a special person. He had been a senator in Oklahoma, was declared a prince of the Native-American Chickasaw Nation and renamed Oklahoma A&M to Oklahoma State University. He became a dear friend, and our relationship became that of a father and son, or at least that's how everyone around us described it. He worked there for me for several years and never took a penny, and he let me know about it frequently. He had sold his business and beautiful home in Dallas so that he and his wife could move into a small house on Alexander to take care of his bedridden mother-in-law. His wife, who was a registered nurse, unfortunately passed away and left him to take care of his mother-in-law until she passed. He gave up a life of leisure to be there for his family and never once complained. From a senator to a guy picking up balls by hand every night out of a field for no pay. Charlie will always hold a special place in my heart. He later passed away in a nursing home with my wife and me as his only visitors. I saw him three times a week for as long as he was there. I kissed him on the forehead one Tuesday night and told him I loved him and that he had fought the good fight and that it was okay to rest. He passed away the next morning. His service was me speaking to about five people, a man who served his country both as a veteran and a senator, a man who helped thousands of people and never asked for anything in return left the world with an old bag of clubs that contained his trashcan pitching wedge and a couple pictures on the wall, all of which reside in my shop to this day. Charlie was my friend from Tishomingo, Oklahoma, whom I owe 126 Dr Peppers due to many late-night chipping contests that I still protest.

Soon the place was quite successful, as were my junior programs, and I was well on my way to being somebody again. I gave a lesson to a gentleman who decided that he should be my partner. He was a successful businessman and could help me do great things there and had more resources than I had. We built a pro shop, a new parking lot, and put in a $20,000 generator to run the lights at night. He introduced me to some great people like Arnold Palmer and Jack Nicklaus. I remember in 1994 playing in Arnold's children's hospital tournament at Bay Hill and afterwards having drinks with Arnold and Winnie. To watch Arnie drink Jack and water and tear up talking about his dog that had passed while Winnie shared stories of his early days as a pilot is something that I'll never forget. Problems soon arose, however, in that my partner never gave the money but rather lent it to the business, and it was expected to be paid back. We spent more than I could make. There were only so many lessons I could give in a day, and that wasn't enough to carry what the golf course was now requiring in order to stay open. I was more than partly responsible for the problem. I had a student trying to make it on the tour, and I frequently caddied for her in events nationwide leaving only Charlie to run the course. Charlie only gave chipping lessons, for which he of course never charged. One winter I decided I could maybe triple my lesson income if I went to Arizona and gave lessons to all the snowbirds, and perhaps that would help. The night before I left, I lay on my living room floor and watched Annette Benning and Warren Beatty in *Love Affair* with my mother-in-law who had cancer. We had a good conversation that night, and I left early the next morning. I had a couple of friends haul me, my 'vette, and my equipment on a trailer to Arizona by way of Las Vegas—that's a story for another time. I hadn't been there two days when my mother-in-law took a turn for the worse and I had to return home. She passed before I arrived. Looking back, I realize I wasn't there for my wife or my mother-in-law when they needed me most. They had given me their total support from the beginning, and I had given only pain in return. It seemed I was making a habit of that.

I soon decided to let the dream of owning my own course go, and I talked the owner of Lake Waco Country Club into letting me build a small building on his range, and in return I would give him half of my junior program earnings. My programs grew, and my teaching status elevated as my students began to do well. Soon I was teaching young people from all over the state. The owner of the club and the course itself weren't doing so well. He decided he needed to develop the range, where my building stood, as a subdivision. I agreed to build a new teaching facility and range at the other end of the course, which his members could use, in return for a long-term lease, and I would keep all I made. That turned out to be a horrible idea on my part. I built a beautiful facility, second to none, with three indoor bays, an indoor putting green, a classroom, and offices. Outside we had practice greens and a beautiful range tee all surrounded by an eighteen-hole par three course as well as an eighteen-hole regulation course. My students were doing awesome: thirty-three individual state and team championships, and over 400 became college golfers. I had my own videotape out, was doing weekly tips for channel 6 and 25, and even covered the Master's tournament in Augusta. We bought a new house near the course, and I was driving a new Corvette. Life was good again. Time for another storm, and it turned out to be in the disguise of a dream come true. The owner was going broke and had decided to sell the course. That meant I could be asked to vacate my facility, which I still had a bank loan on or be required to pay some astronomical fee to stay there by the new owners. I had but one choice, and that was to purchase the facility myself. Two and a half million dollars, that's what he wanted. He agreed to finance $2 million if I could give him $500,000 cash. How could I come up with that money? Well, turns out it wasn't hard. I sold lifetime memberships for $10,000 each and borrowed $50,000 each from five of my friends, most of which had to be paid back with $20,000 interest per loan. The club wasn't worth $1 million much less $2.5 million, but as always, I felt I could make it work. I now owned the country club where I had once served as a bag room boy.

I was able to repay all the people I had to borrow money from to make the down payment, and my micromanaging personality had it all working quite well. We were making money. The previous owner owed a million dollars less on the club than what I had to buy it for, and the course was in horrible shape when I took over. Now the course was immaculate with a beautiful teaching facility, newly renovated restaurant and pool, and new carts. The grounds were kept perfect mainly because my wife and I began to do a lot of the mowing. At times, we would mow till 3 a.m. We worked hard to make the place nice.

This took me away from my academy. Fortunately, one of my former students, Jon Antunes, was now working with me, and he took over the academy with the same passion I had run it with, so it continued to do well. All was well with my soul, and again, I had made myself into somebody. In 2007, I found myself living the dream. I purchased two yachts at Lake Travis, a Sea Ray 420 sedan bridge at the Hollows, and a 2001 Carver 50-footer at Carlos and Charlies. I owned a beautiful small ranch in Crawford with a private teaching facility out back by the pool, a country club with a restaurant, a new Corvette, my wife had a new hummer H2 SUT, and I had a new Ford F250 4X4. I built a stage out by the pool at the club and had parties with live music, many of the performers being friends of mine. Seems I had found blue skies.

However, 2007 also brought some hints of rain on my parade, starting with a flood. The Army Corps of Engineers backed water into my course and held it there to protect residences downstream from being flooded. This flooded my teaching facility and covered at least two-thirds of the course with water and debris. I had to close part of the restaurant and use it as my teaching facility, so we would have some income. When the water receded, we were left with dead greens and a course full of debris, anything from old boats to park dumpsters and driftwood. With little to no income and extremely high gas prices from Hurricane Katrina, we were in a bad way. It was impossible to make payments with no income. We began the process of the cleanup, and just as we did, the previous owner tried to take the property back because he was still a lien holder. Yeah, the property was in bad shape, but he had made a million dollars on selling it to me and looked to take it back and do the same thing again. I had to get an attorney and eventually file bankruptcy to keep him from doing so. Gradually, we were recovering and then another hint of rain; Obama was elected president and promised to tax the rich and reform healthcare just as the markets crashed, and what little membership I had was halved in a matter of days. We held on and continued to press forward. There is a lot more I could say about this time in my life, but I am having trouble with one of the keys on my keypad—the letter I is sticking.

Our 2005 Sea ray 420 Sedan Bridge

Chapter 10

Hello, Ray, It's God.
Do You Have a Minute?

2008–2010

I must admit that I didn't think things could get worse than they were in 2008. Recovering from a flood as well as a court battle over the course, to say I was a bit stressed is an understatement. It's funny how when things are going well in our lives we don't spend much time talking to the Lord. I mean, after all, there's no reason to. We're making good money, family is doing great, health is good, and everything is great. It's when we have problems that we tend to give God a shout. We are willing to spend a lot of time with the Lord when we're in need and very little of our time with the Lord when we're not. The Lord, however, sometimes really wants to talk to us, and I believe that with all my heart. God loves us the way I love my grandson, with a love that undefinable. He loves each one of us that way regardless of our sins; he'd rather we didn't sin, and as a parent he wants us all to accept his love through Christ. Sometimes he allows us to find ourselves in a storm, and I think mostly because he knows that's when we are most likely to call for him. I have been through some bad storms, and I've always come out of them wiser and closer to the Lord. His book says it best in II Corinthians 12: 7-10 (ESV):

> So to keep me from becoming conceited because of the surpassing greatness of the revelations, a thorn was given me in the flesh, a messenger of Satan to harass me, to keep me from becoming conceited. [8] Three times I pleaded with the Lord about this, that it should leave me. [9] But he said to me, "My grace is sufficient for you, for my power is made perfect in weakness." Therefore, I will boast all the more gladly of my weaknesses, so that the power of Christ may rest upon me. [10] For the sake of Christ, then, I am content with weaknesses, insults, hardships, persecutions, and calamities. For when I am weak, then I am strong.

One day while shopping with my wife and my young son, Trevor, in a Target store, God gave me a call. *"Hey, Ray, it's God. Do you have a minute?"* You see, Trevor and I were chasing each other around when I felt something in my chest that was not right. I could barely breathe, and my heart seemed to have lost its ability to beat properly. I found my wife and urged her to take me to the hospital right across the street. I guess she could tell by my face, so she wasted no time in doing so. They made us sit in the waiting room until my wife convinced them that I was really having problems. Once they got me to a room and hooked up to a monitor, several doctors gave me a visit. "We need to stop your heart and restart it," one said. I responded as would any normal person would: "What is plan B?" "There is no plan B; your heart is struggling to find a rhythm."

The thing is, when God calls you must answer the phone; that's his rule. The next day they had me scheduled with a cardiologist, Dr. Michael Attas, who is a good friend of mine to this day. Dr. Attas said I had an arrhythmia and started me on several medications including cholesterol meds, blood pressure meds, and arrhythmia meds. I was skinny and an athlete. How could I have high blood pressure and high cholesterol? I wasn't sure how I got there, but I was in a storm again.

During those next few months, God and I spoke frequently. I began attending church again and trying to be a better person. Things got better, and as time passed, I quit calling God and went back to my normal life. Everything was okay now. Not too much time passed before God called again. Seems we hadn't finished our last conversation. The heart problem was back and worse than before. Dr. Attas referred me to a group of doctors in Austin that specialized in the kind of problems I was having. After one of those doctors performed a surgery on me again things got better, and again my conversations with the Lord dwindled. Funny thing about God is that He is persistent, and so once again He called, and this time He felt our conversation should be longer. The heart thing was back with a vengeance, and so they brought in a specialist to fix it. They placed me in St. David's hospital in Austin, but for some reason my surgery kept getting bumped back. After three days in the hospital with my heart out of rhythm I contracted the flu, and they decided they couldn't do the surgery, and I was sent home. This time God really wanted to talk, and this time I was listening. I was lost and in a bad way. Remembering that David Toms, a golf pro, once had to be airlifted out of the tour championship at East Lake on TV for similar heart problems, I gave him a call. He was doing great and insisted the Mayo Clinic was the answer. I was fortunate enough to get an appointment with Dr. Friedman at the Mayo Clinic a couple weeks later. Because my wife had missed so much work already, my good friend Joel Williamson and I made the drive to Rochester, Minnesota. They put me through a battery of tests for several days, and I truly felt as though I would die. I couldn't take any meds during the series of tests. Joel set up with me every night encouraging me to hang in there. I couldn't have made it through without his help. Finally, Dr. Friedman gave me the results and explained that my case was quite unique, but he felt confident he could help me. He said there was about a 65% chance I could live a relatively normal life and only about 35% that things could go wrong. At that point, I didn't care about odds—I wanted it to be over. I was disappointed when he put me on some different meds to get me by and sent me home. He felt I needed to get things in order, allow him to prepare his plan, and that I should bring my wife back in a month and he would do the surgery. Not at all what I wanted to hear. This time God wanted me to call him frequently and wasn't accepting no for an answer.

That month seemed like a lifetime, and when the day finally came for us to leave, I remember going into my office. Since I had God on speed dial, I called him and asked a favor. "Lord," I said, "Allow me to open this Bible and place a finger on a verse that lets me know that you are hearing me. I am scared for probably the first time in my life. Please just give me a sign that things are going to be fine." With great anticipation, I opened the Good Book and placed my finger down with my eyes shut. When I opened them, I was more than frustrated and immediately called him back. I had placed my finger on a verse in Job, and no way was that going to give me any peace. I needed something uplifting and definite. "Please, Lord," I cried. "Please speak to me to let me know it will be okay." As I began to pick up my finger and give it another try, a word under my finger caught my eye. The word was "speak." I had placed my finger on Job chapter 33 verse 31, which read: ***"Pay attention, Job, and listen to me. Be quiet, and I will speak."*** That verse wasn't God speaking to Job; it was God speaking to me, and I became silent inside and out.

Cheryl and I traveled to Minnesota in my truck. I couldn't fly for a specified time after the operation. Rochester was beautiful with about six feet of snow everywhere; my wife loved it. One of my fellow college golfers, Scott Skogen, now a minister, made the trip over from Wisconsin to pray with me. When they came to take me to surgery, I kissed my wife and told her I loved her. I remember the operating room as if it were yesterday, Big screen monitors above me and to one side, bright lights directly above me, people in masks everywhere, extremely cold since I was naked, and monitors making all kinds of noises. Everyone around me carried on as if I weren't there. I felt alone at the time, and then I heard the voice of Dr. Friedman. "Hello, William, we are about to start. Do you have any questions?" "No, sir," I replied, although I had a million. "Don't worry, everything will be fine." Then the anesthesiologist asked me if I was ready, and I immediately said, "No, wait." *Was I ready* took on a whole new meaning. Yes, I was ready to get my heart fixed. Yes, I was ready to get back to my normal life. But more importantly, for the first time in my life, no, I wasn't ready to answer to God if things went wrong. This time I called God, and He was expecting it. I know because He answered on the first ring. I explained how lost I had been and asked for Him to understand and forgive me. In a calm voice full of love, He said, "I already have, just rest." I looked at the anesthesiologist and said, "Yes, I am ready." I knew if I had spent my last day on earth that I would spend eternity in heaven.

I remember the doctor waking me up during the surgery and asking me questions. While doing so, they put an eight-inch by eight-inch see-through Band-Aid looking thing on my chest, and one of the nurses pulled out a long straw made of stainless steel and started towards my chest. "Do not stick that in me" are the last words I remember before waking up again with it in my chest filled with wires. Again, I was asked questions, and then I awoke with some nurses pushing down on both my groin areas with what seemed like 500 pounds of pressure. What felt like about two minutes from the time they put me to sleep till now had been thirteen hours. When I saw my wife enter the room, she said everything went well, but at that moment it didn't feel that way. I hurt everywhere, and they kept giving me meds that seemed like they worked for about twenty minutes at a time. It's hard to say, but at that moment I missed the clarity I had before I said I was ready, and a part of me almost wished…well, you know. After all, I was ready at that point. What if I lost that along the rest of my journey?

Two days later, Cheryl and I drove 1,000 miles back to Texas in a snowstorm. We just made it through Oklahoma City when behind us they closed the interstate—and by the way, I drove.

As we got closer to Texas, the storm cleared. My storm also cleared. I was alive, my heart was better, and my soul was better. When I look back, I'm glad God and I had that talk. I knew the rest of the journey would still have ups and downs, but I was beginning to think maybe I wasn't alone. Maybe I was never alone. Maybe, just maybe, he was watching me when I was four in my swing just outside the green house on the red dirt road.

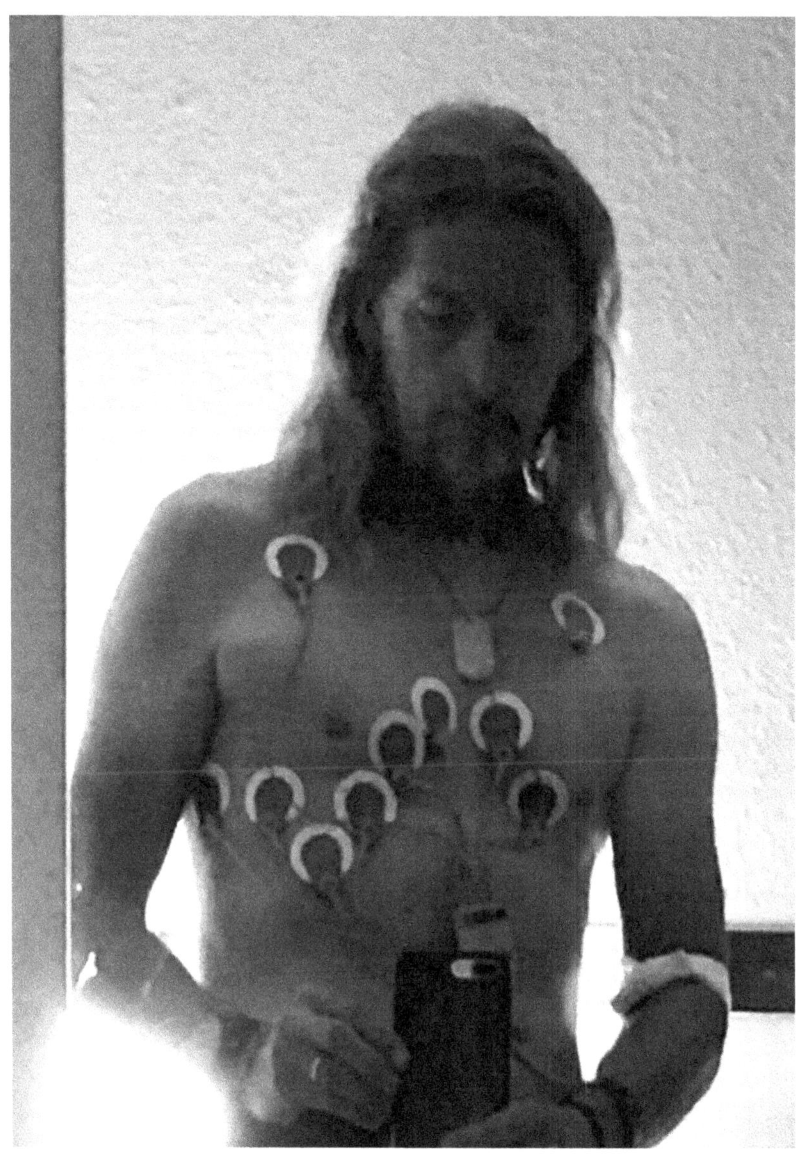

Me at The Mayo Clinic

Chapter 11

More Rain Than Expected

2010–2012

In my life I had experienced some rain, but this was a bit more than expected. In 2008 I began to have heart issues that lasted through 2010. During that time, I was also in a battle with the city. They were using unlimited resources paid for with my tax dollars to keep the local city-owned golf course immaculate and charging me out the wazoo for those same resources. For example, we got a fresh water bill one month for $7,000, and it turned out to be a leak in a water fountain on the course. At the same time, the city course was watering their entire course with fresh city water, and their bill was $0. It should have been more than $200,000 for a month's use in comparison. We found out through an open records request asked for when they refused to adjust my bill. Also, I was paying taxes, more than $48,000 per year, and they paid none. The city course was losing up to $800,000 a year and keeping their facility pristine. I was constantly made aware of the fact that my course was horrible compared to theirs by my members who accused me constantly of mismanaging funds. For a while I tried to explain I could only invest into the course the amount of revenue it was taking in, and if they would play and pay their bills, things would greatly improve. All this fell on deaf ears.

There were many other things in my life going on that made me tired and frustrated. I had three sons, and one was struggling in many ways. I prayed a lot for him and asked God to intervene, which He did. What we ask for doesn't always come in pretty paper and with a bow, but it came nonetheless, and to this day I am thankful for its arrival. My son is doing great and makes me proud to be his father. He takes wonderful care of my beautiful granddaughter, loves our Father in heaven, and calls his mother every day. He is a blessing to me.

In 2012, after a long, hard fight, I decided to give the club back to the lien holders. I had lost both my yachts, my Corvette, and most of my assets trying to save that club, and it was time to let it go. You would think I would be consumed by anger, but I wasn't. I simply moved on. I had a better appreciation of how storms worked after God and I started communicating on a more regular basis in 2010.

One of the lien holders, the majority lien holder, not the one who tried to take the club back in 2007-8, was a decent guy. His dad, whom I originally dealt with, had passed away, and he had inherited the deed. I offered him $1.5 million, which was a number I thought I could make work, but he felt it was worth more. He asked if I would help manage the place until he could sell it, and I agreed if I could keep using my building, which he agreed to. The members, who always thought they knew more than anyone else about running a business, decided to buy it. They worked out a short-term deal with him and worked out a deal with me to rent my equipment. I wasn't always the sharpest knife in the drawer, but I wasn't the dullest either. I started a new company when I purchased the club and put all the equipment in that company because I was forced to buy it separately from the purchase of the club. I charged them exactly what my payments were monthly; in return, I continued to use my building free of charge. This was a good deal for us both. Soon they realized they were wrong about my mismanaging of funds and that there was no way they could make enough to pay the bills; hence, the first person they quit paying was me. I explained to them that the equipment had to be paid for monthly, or it would be picked up by those I was buying it from. They then wrote me a formal letter stating that I didn't own the equipment, that it was and always had been owned by the club. When I confronted them, they informed me it was strictly business not personal and that I was welcome to continue to use the building. I knew that soon they would not be able to pay any bills and would lose the club, so I hired an attorney. When I brought them the papers demanding payment, I also assured them that it wasn't personal but just business. Their response wasn't as calm as mine, and they said they wanted me off the premises within a week. After discussing this with my attorney, we decided to impound the equipment until a settlement was reached. The day they drove down to my teaching facility to ask me to leave is the same day that the constable arrived to impound the equipment. Handing me a paper, the member representative told me that this was now personal and to leave before they called the cops, to which I replied, "Here is a paper as well that I'd like to give you. It simply states that I am leaving, but I'm taking my things with me. And by the way, to me, it's still not personal."

I rode back up to the pro shop with the constable. We walked in, and he said, "Everybody, put everything down, step back away from the register, and please do so immediately." We emptied the register on the floor and gave them the tape. In the parking lot were five big rigs with trailers. A workforce of employees came in, and they took everything that wasn't attached to the wall and some things that were, the counter, the chairs, the TV, the register, everything. There was not a piece of anything left in the room. They loaded up all the golf carts, all the equipment, everything in the maintenance barn—every piece of equipment on that property that was mine was loaded on the trucks. Then we went to the restaurant and asked everyone to stand up and step away from the table, and we took every plate, every dish, every utensil, every glass—every piece of equipment was loaded from freezers to coffeemakers. I had been smart enough to build a small teaching facility in my backyard, so I still had a place to teach, and they allowed Jon Antunes to run those programs and pay them to use the building.

I finally won in court because I found a text from the owner that read, *"Ray, when are you going to pay the property taxes on all the equipment? It's not mine; it belongs to you, and so do the taxes."* That text, and the fact that all that equipment was in a different company name and that I had been paying property taxes on that separate from the Lake Country Club ever since I owned it, gave me the victory. I must say, I'm not sure it was a victory. By the time I paid my attorneys, I had very little money left from the sale of the equipment considering what I had in it. Oh well, it's just paper and ink. I looked at it as if God were saying to me, "I am shutting a door but will soon open another." I had learned that storms were a necessary part of my adventure and that there would surely be a rainbow on the other side. I needed a break from golf and from the lifestyle I had been living. Maybe it was time for me to turn my attention from fairways to fields.

Chapter 12

From Fairways to Fields

I spent a good deal of my life trying to acquire wealth thinking, I guess, that that would make me happy. I had done so, and it didn't. As quickly as it came, it also went, and for whatever reason I was okay with it. I was tired of fighting the world, tired of trying to prove my self-worth—in general, I was just tired. Deep down I knew I would find a way back, but now I wasn't in a hurry. Every soldier needs a day away from the battle, and I needed mine.

I spent much of my life either playing golf or teaching others to do so. I wore nice clothes, drove expensive cars, stayed at nice resorts, and flew all over the country, many times in private jets. I had owned not one but two yachts, a country club complete with restaurant and teaching facility, a small ranch in Crawford, and pretty much did anything I wanted. I had come a long way and had a life that many envied. Things aren't always what they appear to be. I worked hard and sacrificed a lot, especially time with my family, to buy those boats, the country club, the fancy cars, and that ranch, and in the end what I had done didn't seem to make any sense. **Did I enjoy those things? Of course, who wouldn't? But I had traded something for them I could never get back. I had traded time, something that you never really know how much you have. It's something that when spent can't be replaced. Looking back, I didn't get much for the price I paid.** Yeah, I made some good friends on D dock at the Hollows Marina that I'm thankful for, but I could've done that with one much smaller boat. I mean, when I really thought about it, all I had worked so hard for now belonged to someone else. I had traded my most prized possession for something that I had no control over. Perhaps I was a little smarter because of it all, but mostly I was just tired.

Although I continued to teach golf at my private teaching facility behind my house and play when the opportunity presented itself, I was slowly turning into a guy who enjoyed riding and racing his bike. There was something about it that was fresh air to my soul.

My son Trevor had introduced me to biking when I was fifty-four years old. He asked me to ride about a mile from our house to the wetlands and back, and so I did. I remember sitting in the chair in our living room and my wife asking if I was okay. My response was real and heartfelt. "I am a far cry from okay; I'm dying." "What is wrong?" she asked, and let me know that I looked terrible. "I just rode a bike with your son to the wetlands and back; the hill coming back almost killed me." She looked at me with confusion and said, "What hill?" With what little breath that remained in me I said, "Cheryl, I could be wrong, but somehow our house is in the middle of the Rockies." I looked like an athlete, and I thought I was in great shape. After all, I had been doing P90X for about a year, and I was all about what I ate, a health nut as described by my wife. I guess there's being in shape, and there's looking good. I'm a bit biased, but I was good at the second and horrible at the first. One of my friends, Mark, from my boat days at Lake Travis, allowed me to borrow a mountain bike he never used. Tommy, also a good friend, whose wife rode and raced a lot, started taking me to the trails. I was hooked.

I started hanging around a small bike shop in town called Bicycles Outback. While hanging out there, I soon became friends with the owner, Larry, and with most of the guys who worked there. Even the shop cat, a female cat also named Larry, got attached to me. Several guys I met at that shop played a huge role in the next couple years of my life, and to this day, although the shop doesn't exist anymore, are still my good friends. Larry still owned the place, but Ian was in the middle of buying it. John and Glenn were the mechanics, Dennis the bike fitter, and Fred the local hero. Each played a role in my becoming a better cyclist. I didn't really care for road biking much and tended to lean more towards the trails. Dennis fit my bikes to me and was strictly a road guy. I rode with his group most every Wednesday morning. In the beginning they would run off and leave me, but John would always come back and lead me home. I loved the trails, and that quickly became my passion. I started racing the TMBRA XC series in central Texas and began to improve quickly. I began as a Cat 2 rider, even though I was a beginner and should have raced Cat 3. Being an athlete my whole life, I had too much pride to call myself a beginner at anything, and so I spent quite a bit of time finishing last in Cat 2. My skills improved quickly, but I just didn't have the legs necessary in twenty-four-mile races to do well.

John talked me into building a single-speed and a fully rigid one at that. He convinced me I would get stronger, learn to handle the bike better, and do so in a much shorter length of time. Jon was a single-speeder, a super strong rider, and he was different than the other guys. I had him build me a Vassago, and I became a single-speed guy myself.

Riding a single-speed is not for everyone, but when it's for you, you know it. It's love at first sight, or maybe lust at first sight—who knows? Like all new relationships, it's hot and steamy, and then it cools off. A relationship in which both parties are headstrong and must be right all the time. No gears, so hills meant get stronger or get off. No shocks, so lines meant pick good ones or get thrown off. Like a cowboy breaking a horse (or as some say, like a horse breaking a cowboy), you eventually come to a compromise. If it's not true love, you go your separate ways, but if it is, you are soulmates for life. A single-speed fit my personality all too well and soon became who I was. I own a couple of $14,000 road and mountain bikes, yet every day I ride my $4,000 single-speed and will until the end. I improved greatly, as Jon said I would, and soon had enough good finishes to become a Cat 1 racer. Now, instead of finishing in the middle of the pack in Cat 2, I could finish near the back of the pack in Cat 1. Didn't matter to me. I was now in the top group regardless of where I finished. In 2015, I won the Marathon series state championship in the Single-Speed Open category, not because I was the best single-speeder in the state but because I was the most persistent. Single-speeds are simple and reliable, and that's something I desperately needed in my life.

Ian and his wife invited us to spend a weekend camping at Reveille Peak with them and another couple. I took my bus, so it really wasn't camping for us, but we were there nonetheless. While sitting around a fire and enjoying a peaceful night under the stars, Ian asked me about golf, and had I ever played in any of the big tournaments like the Masters or the US Open, to which I replied, "No, but I sure would like to." I had played almost every course those guys played except for Augusta. I asked Ian what the main mountain bike races in the sport were. For example, in golf the four majors include the Masters, US Open, British

Open, and the PGA championship. Did they have major races like that in mountain biking? Ian replied, "Well, I guess there are a few that everyone puts on their bucket list. The Tour Divide, of course, Leadville, the Whiskey 50, 24 Hours Old Pueblo, all a must, and perhaps the Dirty Kanza as well." I of course replied, "I'm going to do every one of those races," to which everyone began laughing, including me. Little did they know in my heart I truly felt like I would do all those races. Ian said we should do Old Pueblo together as a team and of course I was all in. After that weekend, I continually tried to get them to follow through, but there was always a reason they couldn't.

For whatever reason I started riding a lot with Fred. Fred was 79 years old and had already won multiple world championships and several national championships—impressive for someone who started riding a mountain bike at age 62. I enjoyed Fred's company and our time together both on and off the bike. Much of what I learned about racing came from Fred and his endless wisdom. We have spent countless hours not only riding the backroads of central Texas but across the Midwest. Although we are much different—I am a Christian, and he's an atheist— we have a common thread. We both respect those who sometimes feel different than ourselves and their right to do so, we both are passionate about what we do, and we are both competitive and willing to push ourselves far beyond our limits.

One night, Fred and his wife Suzanne invited my wife and me over to watch a movie titled *24 Hours*. It was about a gentleman, Chris Eatough, who had won six world championships in twenty-four-hour racing and was trying to win his seventh. I was impressed a guy could ride a bike for twenty-four straight hours and immediately wondered if I could do that. I soon signed up for my first twenty-four-hour race in Smithville, Texas—24 Hours at Rocky Hill. I loved it and was hooked, partly because I did better than I ever did in a one-and-a-half-hour race. Turns out, I wasn't fast but could ride for a long time. First thing I did when I got home was to sign up for 24 Hours of Ole Pueblo, one of Ian's must-do races. Before I knew it, I was in a little makeshift town in the dessert just outside of Tucson, Arizona, and ready to race my first 24 Hours of Ole Pueblo. A good friend of mine, Tommy Billeaud, rode with me to Arizona. We took my truck and my Airstream and had quite the experience getting it parked at the venue. I place most of the blame on Coach. At one point my truck was in a position where the right front tire was about three feet off the ground, and the left was buried in the fender well. Looking back, it was funny seeing a crowd of people there to watch a bike race watching us park a twenty-eight-foot Airstream pulled by a Ford F250 in a spot on a mountain designed to accommodate a Volkswagen Beetle. Not as funny as the look on Coach's face after he decided to ride a practice lap with me and we topped the second of seven hills appropriately named "the bitches." Once he caught his breath, he informed me that he and Jesus were close as he climbed the hill. I asked how close, and he replied, "A breath away from meeting in person." Good times. After racing all day and night in the desert with the stars as big as basketballs, I knew I was on to something. The first part of the loop was some great single-track through the desert, which just had a beautiful flow to it, and at the end you had a three-mile climb up the backside of a mountain and then dropped into the makeshift town of Ole Pueblo. The town consisted of tents and RVs with campfires everywhere. The people were up all night cheering us on as we made our way through the makeshift streets and back to the start of the loop. Truly an unbelievable experience. I've done Ole Pueblo four times, and it's still one of my favorite races. One race marked off the bucket list.

Later that year I raced 24-Hour Nationals in Gallup, New Mexico. I finished fifteenth and perhaps could have done better had I not gotten frustrated with the race officials and just called it a day with about eight hours left. We had lots of rain after the first four hours of the race, and conditions quickly deteriorated. One lap I must have walked (and in some places crawled) three-quarters of the lap, but I finished it. Some people got off the lap where it passed near a road and simply took the road back to the start. Race officials had a hard time determining who did what, so they canceled that lap for everyone and suspended the race temporarily to see if things would get better. I protested, but to no avail, so I just packed up and left. Patience is not one of my better traits.

When I raced Ole Pueblo, I fell in love with the desert. Ian had mentioned the Whiskey 50, which is held in Prescott, Arizona, so I signed up. Man, what a great race! It's the best purse for any mountain bike race in the country, so it draws some big names. The town of Prescott really goes all out to make it a special weekend with nightly bands and parties, just amazing. The race itself is one of the most fun races I've ever done, and the track is awesome, about twenty-six miles of sweet and technical single-track with a twelve-mile out and back. The weather was superb, and before I knew it race number two on Ian's list was in the books. I liked the Whiskey so much that I have raced it every year but one since that time. I finally talked Fred into doing it—he just got tired of me telling him how good the race and weather were—so he signed up. That year was a bit different. When Fred and I reached the start line it was a bit chilly and looked like rain. I had never seen that before, and by the time we hit the woods it was a full-blown snowstorm. Fred was unable to finish due to his hands, and most who had not reached a certain point were turned back. I was one of the lucky ones who finished. Fred still rides with me, believe it or not.

If you've ever been in a relationship that you knew was bad for you but just couldn't let it go, then you understand the relationship I have with one race, Leadville. In 2012 I qualified for Leadville for the first time via the Leadville Camp of Champions. As I soon learned, Leadville would be the toughest race for me to do—104 miles with 13,000 feet of climbing at 10-13.000 feet in altitude. Leadville is more of a road race than a mountain bike race with some tough climbs but nothing too technical. With a resting heart rate of between 33 and 40 and a maximum heart rate of about 130, I'm just not built to do this race. Before I left for Leadville, all the bike friends wished me luck and made sure I understood it was the experience of just being there that matters— i.e., *"It's too tough, you have no chance, so don't be disappointed."* When I arrived all I could think of was, *"Man this is beautiful,"* and *"Wow, it's hard to breathe up here."* Fred and I had a great time riding the course together and pushing each other, and the weather was perfect. On race day I started out well and surprised myself by making the cut at Twin Lakes outbound and then again at Twin Lakes inbound. The last cut is at the pipeline feed station at mile 80, and I missed that one by about fifteen minutes. I was disappointed because I knew my time from there in would have been good enough for a buckle. I was much too cautious coming down columbine, and it cost me. I took the road back to town and found Suzanne near the finish line. I asked about Fred, and she said he might have a chance. There was only about thirteen minutes left, so I ran up 6th Street to where the riders entered from the boulevard and waited. When Fred got to that point he was spent, and looked it, but he had like four minutes to get to that red carpet, and so I did what anyone would do: I started pushing him with all my might. He made it, he got a buckle, and he did it at seventy-nine years of age—the oldest man ever to do so. It was awesome, and I was there to see it. I have raced Leadville every year but one since and have only crossed that red carpet once.

Every year I race Leadville something bad happens in my life. One year I developed the worst sinus infection ever and didn't make the last gate, and another year my wife and I had sold our home bought a new home and had started renovating it just a couple days before the race. The guy who bought our house was a well-respected businessman and was out of town, but he had to have the house vacant for his renovators on a certain date. The closing was set accordingly. Since I had to leave for Leadville and he hadn't made it back, the bank allowed all parties to finish closing, and it would complete upon his signature. The people who owned the house we were buying allowed us to move in, so we did and began the renovations. I headed to Leadville late, and the day before the race the man buying our house was arrested by the FBI, and all his accounts were frozen. My wife called in tears. I started the race the next morning but had to withdraw and go home—mentally, I was spent. Luckily, the people let us out of the deal with the other house with the exception we were out the money for the renovations we had made. Another year my wife decided to go and take our four dogs. She hated being there and decided she wanted to go home two days before the race, so I drove her a thousand miles back to Texas and then drove a thousand miles back; I didn't have a good race. The year I crossed the red carpet I had made the last split with a ton of time to spare, and as I was climbing Powerline it poured and the trail became slippery and muddy.

It caused me to have to walk and be cautious in many places, and I missed the buckle by about thirteen minutes. Finally, the last try ended when my wife was hospitalized a couple days before the race and I had to return home. This was to be the year, an individual time trial across Texas, 1,029 miles on a single-speed the month before, would get me in great shape, and then I would straight to Leadville. I completed the Race Across Texas after being hit by a car during the race. Somehow, I managed to finish. After the race I had several medical appointments to see how bad my injuries were. Turns out, several surgeries put Leadville out of the picture for 2018.

This year, 2019, will be mine as well as Fred's last year there, Maybe, just maybe, one of us will find silver. Even if I don't, that's three races on Ian's list completed.

I always invited students to go ride with me, and they usually did. I took Mathew Watson to both the Whiskey and Leadville. Another student, Frankie Alinson, and I raced the San Juan Hut 200 together and won. I had begun to figure out what I liked most was the long races, more for the money you might say. I just didn't have the speed to compete in short races, but I loved them. I remembered Ian talking about the Dirty Kanza, which was a 200-mile race that began and ended in Emporia, Kansas. My mechanic at the time, Mat Bates, and Fred both had signed up, so I did as well. Of course, I picked the hardest year in the race's history. Rebecca Rush said later she wanted something to go wrong with her bike, so she could quit. My good friend Yuri Hauswald won the race in just over fourteen hours. Mud and wet conditions caused the race to lose more riders than not; both Fred and Mat had to stop. This bad luck for most was good for me. I wasn't fast, but I knew I could ride steady for twenty-four hours because I had done it. I finished, and before I knew it race number four was completed.

I loved cycling so much that I started a program at Baylor University where I taught four mountain bike classes and two road bike classes, and I wrote the book that all those classes used titled *Cycling 101*. This wasn't my first experience writing books. I had written four golf books, which Baylor and other schools used for their golf classes, but this book was fun. One thing I had learned was that some races are better suited for some riders than others. I was a distance guy, and soon that's where my focus would turn. I had completed four of the five races Ian mentioned with only the Tour Divide left, and I knew I would soon attempt that one as well. A lot had changed in my life. I had gone from playing in lush fairways to riding in rough trails, but I was looking forward to some peaceful fields and maybe, just maybe, a few less storms.

Arnold Palmer and I in 1994

Me racing a 24 hour at old Pueblo in Arizona

Chapter 13

God's Second Greatest Gift (Grandson)

There is no question in my mind that God's greatest gift to this world was his son, Jesus Christ. Although many of my friends disagree with me and don't believe in God, I always remember a line I heard once that basically says that that's okay because He believes in them. In fact, He believes in them so much that he allowed his son to be crucified for sins He never committed. He provided a path for those of us who are lost, and it's much easier to read than my Garmin. I never truly understood how great a gift that was because I never truly understood love. As I've said before, I'm not sure I ever loved anyone with the love I now know exists. A love that is so strong that it occupies every fiber in your body, controls your thoughts 24-7, and can make you smile and cry at the same time. A love that makes you want to be better. That understanding arrived June 2, 2014.

I have the most awesome grandchildren in the world. Alex came first, followed by Gabe, courtesy of my oldest son, Shannon, and his wife, Kim. Then came Kallie, also a beautiful young lady, courtesy of my middle son, Nick, and his wife, Ashley, and finally my grandson Kash, courtesy of my youngest son, Trevor, and his wife, Jennifer. Every grandchild I have is a poster child for "Best Grandchild Ever." I have been truly blessed. Kash was different than the rest in that he lived in the same town as we did. He spent a lot of time at our house when he was a baby and even more as he grew into a toddler. I taught him to crawl, to walk, to drink out of a straw, and, most importantly, to ride a bike at age two. I held him up in front of the TV and watched football with him, pushed him in a stroller to the end of our property and back many times, and gave him rides on all my bikes when he wasn't much bigger than my seat bag. I was even there when he lost his first tooth. We were riding bikes late at night playing a game of chase, and as he was looking back to tell me he had won. He ran into my wife's parked Hummer face-first. I ran to him, and he was holding his mouth but not crying. When I grabbed him, I said, "Grandson, let me see." When he moved his hand and I saw his tooth, tears filled my eyes. "Grandad, is it bleeding," he said, and about that time he saw the blood on his hand and we both were crying. I remember feeling like I'd let him down by letting him get hurt, and I was devastated. My thought was, *"How am I going to protect him his whole life when I'm old and may not be here?"* That was a thought that had never entered my mind before, and I had three grown boys. To say I had been lost my entire life was an understatement.

Many days when he was a just baby I would go to his house and take him across the street to their neighborhood playground, and we would just swing. One day when I was leaving his mom was holding him up to the glass door to say bye, and he did something strange. He placed his hand on the door and looked straight at me, I placed mine on the outside of the door so that it covered his and he smiled the biggest smile ever. We became inseparable and are to this day. Rarely do we leave each other's company without our arms around each other in tears. If there is such a thing as a soulmate, he is mine. I can't imagine a life without him in it, without holding his hand or talking to him about the craziest of crazy things. A life without us watching dinosaur videos, *Paw Patrol, or Ranger LB* or riding our bikes to all hours of the night, without the hugs and the sloppy kisses. For the first time in my life I had a purpose, a reason to exist. It was God's way of showing me all that I had allowed to pass through my fingertips and a second chance to show Him I could do it right. **When no one in the world had ever been able to soften a heart so hardened by life that its beats were scattered, to settle a soul destined to be unsettled, to open eyes that had been glued shut, to replace a seasoned anger with a calming trust, to fill an emptiness with an undying love, Grandson did so with just one look**. He gave me a reason to change, a reason to do more than exist, a reason to trust someone other than myself. He taught me what true love was, and in doing so he showed me just how special God's gift to us is. I now know God's love is undefinable, extremely precious, and undeserved by us all. As far as Kash, well, he knows that he's loved, and in his heart he believes his Grandad will always be there for him. He trusts me with all his heart and soul and feels the same bond that I feel. I know that to be true by the way he holds me when we sleep, by the look in his eyes when we see each other after a day or so apart, and by the softness of his words when he says, "I love you, Grandad." **His childhood will be filled with adventure, with love, and with trust because I never want him to get from there to here the way I did.** When he watches my

Tour Divide videos and looks at my pics from all my races, he always tells me the same thing, "Grandad, you were never scared because I was always right behind you." To this day, I have no idea why he says that, but somehow and for some reason, I believe him.

To say we have spent a lot of time playing together is an understatement. In our time together playing in the huge sand pile just behind the house, taking long walks in the woods looking for "Big Bad," upstairs playing with the gazillion toys he has accumulated, riding bikes to all hours, and most importantly those conversations we have while snuggled up in bed just before sleep takes him away from me, I've come to appreciate the great gift that children have. To Grandson everything is an adventure filled with excitement and promise. When things don't go as planned, he is somewhat disappointed but only for a short time. Then it's on to the next adventure. There's never a reason to believe that it won't work out. He always has everything he needs to live out his adventures, even when all he has is the diaper he's wearing (or many times not wearing). He is content when he closes his eyes, and his first words in the morning are always, "Grandad, the sun is up. It's time to play." Most importantly, he believes he can do anything, and he believes it with all his heart and soul. As adults we have that same gift; it's just that we seem to have misplaced it somewhere along the way. Everyday life seems to encourage us to put away those childhood beliefs. There's no way we have all we need to get by; there are lots of things we will never be able to do. Being content is a fairy tale, and the only adventure we have is trying to make it month to month. Happiness is defined by wealth, possessions, lack of struggle, and such. I lived some fifty-five years of my life with that gift hidden away, and then one day while riding a bike in the middle of nowhere I found it. Now I carry it with me just as my grandson does, and I made a promise to myself never to lose it again.

I have spent many sleepless nights because of Grandson, mostly recording our time together in print so that if something happens to me while he is young, he will someday be able to read my print and hear my voice and know how much he is loved. Below are a few examples:

The words of a child

It's such a simple language, that of a child.
It can make the toughest man cry and the saddest man smile.
To understand, one doesn't have to be smart.
If you listen, you'll get it because it comes from their heart.

"Dandad, how are you? Come on, come on, hurry, hand."
I love you, Grandad, and right now you're my best friend,
So hurry, let's go play. There's so much we need to do.
There's rocks to be stacked, bikes to be rode, and concrete to write on too.

Up and down the stairs, then outside to play in water.
Come on, Grandad, I'm a little boy now no longer a toddler.
Then later there are bubbles and a shower,
Making a watery mess that will take an hour.

There's so much to do, and we have so little time.
My cup, my puppies of two, and put on my favorite nursery rhyme.
Sit by me, Grandad, and don't let me go.
Mommy and Daddy will be coming soon, you know.

"No, Dandad, no," I don't want to go. "Okay, okay," I'll be back again.
Mommy and Daddy already know that you're my very best friend.
"I wuv you, Dandad." God said to tell you hi.
He knows you love me too and says its okay
if we both sometimes cry.

Conversations with my Grandson
His remarks are in quotations

Hey, Grandson.
"What you doing, Grandad?"
I'm just sitting here thinking 'bout you.
"Hey, you wanna, you wanna go upstairs and play with me?"
Let's do it, Grandson, nothing better I'd like to do.

"Hey, Grandad."
What's up, Grandson?
"You wanna go ride our bikes?"
Which one you going to ride, the red or the green one?
"It's the blue one, Grandad, that I really like."

Hey, Grandson, what happen to your clothes?
"Grandad, the po po going to come get me?"
I won't let them, Grandson.
Even the po po know we gotta go outside to pee.

"Hey, Grandad, where you at?"
Right here, Grandson, getting something to drink.
"Grandad, I don't like it when you do that."
Do what, Grandson?
"I don't like it when you leave."

Hey, Grandson.
"Where you going, Grandad?"
I going to feed the chickens, just take me a little while.
"I going to come with you, Grandad."
Grandson, you just want to play in that crazy dirt pile.

"Hey, Grandad."
What's up, Grandson?
"You wanna watch a video with me?"

Let me guess, you wanna watch the dinosaur one.
"Come lay down by me, and you see."

Hey, Grandson.
"What you doing, Grandad?"
I wanna go see if we can find "Big Bad."
"Let me get my stick, and I come with you, Grandad."
Grandson, I think you can take him, especially when you're mad.

"Hey, Grandad."
Yes, Grandson?
"You wanna be my friend?"
I'd like that, Grandson, more than anything.
"Okay, Grandad, you my berry best friend."

Hey, Grandson.
"What you want, Grandad?"
You wanna watch a video with me, Grandson?
"Hey, Grandad, you wanna watch rum pum pum?"
Let's do it.
"That's my favorite one."

"Hey, Grandad, you love me."
More than you will ever know, Grandson.
"Hey, Grandad, I be really good."
You're always good, but they will still make you go, Grandson.

"I stay here with you, Grandad.
You lay real close to me.
You make me sad, Grandad.
Get under here, and no one can see."

"Grandad, come on, I show you."
Grandson, I wish I knew what to do.
"No one can see us. See, I told you"
Grandson, you don't know how much I wish that were true.

"You wanna go upstairs and play with my toys?"
"Let's race. I gonna win; don't get mad."
Grandson, you can do this. You are a big boy.
"I not that big, Grandad."

"No, no, Grandad. We win together."
Okay, Grandson, that sounds like a good deal.
"We can play here forever."
If I were magic, Grandson, I'd make that real.

"I love you, Grandad."
I love you, Grandson.
"Sometimes I can't hear you, Grandad."
Close your eyes. I'm right here, Grandson.

Some of my favorite sayings

See, I told you. What you doing, Grandad? I go with you. I really strong. You not listening to me, Grandad. Wait for me, Grandad. Wanna play with me, Grandad? Let's show Grandma our poopy butts. I want Donald's, wanna watch a video, I stay with you Grandad, You love me Grandad. You hear me, Grandad. Don't leave me, Grandad. It's all better Grandad, you make me sad, Aww, Jake, I not gonna talk to you, You not going to leave me, Grandad. Hey, wait for me. Kick it, Grandad, I do it. That not very nice. I stay at Grandad's house, You wanna go upstairs? You going to jail. Hey, matey, Granger LB, I chunk your cheese. I love you, Grandad. You my friend, let's share, we win together, I gonna make it all better. Hey, Grandad, hey Grandad, hey Grandad, I show you something. Good morning, Grandad, the sun is up.

Grandson and I and when he was just under 2

Chapter 14

Race Across Texas 2014

As I look back, I believe the change I speak of began with the Race Across Texas in 2014. This was the first real adventure on a bike for me. When I first signed up for this race, I really had no idea what I was getting myself into. A race from Texarkana, Arkansas, to Tucumcari, New Mexico, about 1,000 miles of mostly trail, didn't sound too tough. Two and a half years ago I had quit playing golf, which is what I had done for a living over the last twenty-five years, and stated riding mountain bikes. During those two and a half years I had raced pretty much every TMBRA series race that was held. I had also raced the Whiskey 50, Leadville 100, and 24 Hours of Ole Pueblo. Never, however, had I raced multiple days in a row, especially when those days were to be 100-plus miles per day. The longest I had ever been on a bike at one time was 230 miles in a twenty-four-hour race with support and on a bike that weighed about twenty-one pounds. A couple of weeks before the RAT I raced the Camino 205, which is an awesome race, so I figured not only was I ready but also that I was probably the favorite to win.☺ Funny thing about getting older, the brain seems to frequently forget that its job is to think logically!

My friend Dave drove me to Texarkana the day before the race was to start. We drove the first three miles of the race leaving town to help me get familiar with the start and make sure my brand-new Garmin Oregon 650T was working properly. Dave, well, he's another story for another time. After getting everything laid out, I rested until the racers' meeting at 8:00 p.m. The meeting was a bit of an eye opener. We discussed the dangers of the race, such as starting the same morning that deer season opened, and the condition of some of the trails, treacherous at night for sure. After listening to the pitfalls as well as everyone's experience levels, I went from thinking I was the favorite to hoping I could finish and not become some drunken hunter's hood ornament along the way!

The night's sleep was exactly like it always is before a big race—nonexistent—and morning came too quickly. I ate my pre-determined breakfast, got dressed, and lined up for what I thought was going to be a big deal—the start. Kevin said good luck, and everyone took their time in just rolling out; it didn't seem like any race I'd ever been in. I was able to stay among the front runners for a long time, and then something I didn't expect to happen happened: my Garmin froze. I stopped and tried to fix it but with no luck. Riders were passing me, and by the time I got back on the road I found myself in the place one doesn't want to be without a working GPS unit, behind the leaders far enough that I couldn't see them and far enough in front of the riders having fun that I couldn't see them either. Much like in life, I was alone, and the only help I had was me.

I followed bike tracks to a town called New Boston. No tracks on pavement, but as fate would have it, I saw a couple riders at a DQ and pulled in. I worked feverishly on my Garmin and got it working, or so I thought. After ordering something to eat I gathered myself and formulated a plan. Originally, I was going to say hi to my sis who worked in New Boston, but I had to scrap that idea. Instead I would simply stay with these guys until the end of the first segment to make sure my GPS was good, and at the check-in I would get out my cue sheets, which I thought I'd never use, and familiarize myself with the next part of the route. I knew at that point I would have to be on my own since I wasn't stopping for the night at that first checkpoint. Two of my grandkids live in Blossom, but they were not in town that day, so there was no reason to tarry. Besides, I couldn't finish in six days unless I were to cover the first three segments in two days. Also, I had lived in Paris, a town to which the route would pass closely, and I wanted to visit an uncle who still lived there.

Along the next seventy miles to Blossom, which served as the end of our first segment, the Garmin froze several times, so I wasn't simply enjoying the ride like I thought I would. I found myself worrying about things I had no control over—pretty much like my everyday life. The route went through the south portion of Paris down Jefferson Road and then cut over to Washington. Jefferson Road…that sounded so familiar. As I rolled along the route, I passed the junior high school and remembered that as being the high school I had attended for half a year as a freshman. Then, as I turned on Jefferson Road, I found myself at an intersection looking right at an old run-down house. It dawned on me that was the last place I had lived with my dad. The route took me not only past the very house but back to a time in my life that I hadn't thought about in a long, long time.

As I stood over my bike and stared at the house, it seemed like only yesterday, and yet it was forty-one years ago. Barely fifteen years of age, after a big fight with my dad, I ran out of that house and became an adult who had to support himself from that moment on. My whole life came rushing back. Overwhelmed with emotions, I just stood there. I could almost see a much younger me running out that door scared yet relieved that it was over. My prayers had been answered, and now I was free. That younger me stopped and stared at the road as if he saw me there, and I couldn't help but think if I could only speak to him even for a moment, what would I say. As he threw gravel leaving that driveway on his way to me, I pushed the pedal over and begin rolling away. Even though I couldn't speak to him, I felt he was speaking to me.

My aunt had just passed away about three months before the race. I promised many times to come see her, but life kept me too busy until the funeral of course. That's why I was going to stop and see my uncle while I was there. In just one moment I went from worrying about getting lost with my GPS acting up to realizing I had been navigating for a long time without one. A calm came over me as I rode through the streets of a town I had lived in for a short time but that had changed my life so dramatically. I turned off the Garmin and proceeded to my uncle's house on the north side of town. After a good visit I headed for Roxton, Texas, where I would spend the first night of the race in a bed-and-breakfast with a fellow racer, Rick Pressor. The cue sheets were easy to read for that part of the segment, and the sunset led to a chilly night, but the end of that day's ride had been sweet. We had the place to ourselves, and the owners were nice enough to leave us a chicken salad in the fridge. I ate, cleaned up, and went to bed.

I replaced the batteries in the Garmin a third time, and it was working again. My focus turned back to riding hard and finishing the second and third segments by the end of the day. Basically, it would be a 170-mile day. We all had reason to press forward due to the forecast of some cold and wet stuff that was a definite. One section of the trail was iffy in good weather but would be virtually impassable in bad. I really wanted to pass that point.

After a good night's rest, I got an early start headed to Arrowhead State Park. My legs felt surprisingly good, as did I. Maybe I could win this race! It was probably my best day thus far on a bike. I felt good, the scenery was good, and my mind still hadn't come back to the reality of what we were doing. My trusty steed and I decided to keep going past Arrowhead State Park and into Wichita Falls for the night. I really wanted to beat the rain to Vernon. The next morning started well. The front had arrived but not in full force, and Vernon was in sight. As the day progressed, the worst became a reality. Wind, rain, and mud made the trail impossible to ride and not very easy to push, which is what I did for most of the day. One thing was for sure: whichever way I was going, it was always into the wind and uphill! I had found the Bermuda Triangle of Northwest Texas. The trail was so bad, but there was no way to get off it. I couldn't just head up some makeshift gravel road because I had no idea where it would lead. Back to real life again; plans hardly ever work the way we want them too. I just did what I had done most of my life; I simply kept moving forward. If I died frozen, wet, and alone out here, so be it. I had made up my mind I was not going to let anything else bother me. It began raining harder, the winds got stronger, the mud thicker, and then came my first flat. I was only a bit pissed. After putting a tube in the rear tire of a bike that weighs sixty-eight pounds in mud with a tire that was clearly smaller than the wheel it was on, one could probably gather I was a tad more pissed than before. I finally made it to a section that I could ride and found a country store to get food and warm up a bit. The elderly man behind the counter (I won't say old for obvious reasons) asked me a good question. He said, "Son, what the hell you doing on a bike in this kind of weather way out here?" I told him about the race, and he replied, "If that don't beat all I ever seen." At that point, I pretty much agreed with him.☺ I pressed on and decided to go all the way to Quanah to get a motel and clean up.

When I got up the next morning, I realized that this was a bit more than I had anticipated, but physically I still felt great. The problem that arose was mental. I now was riding to finish, and suddenly I became aware of my Strada Cateye and the miles ticking by. For the first time, I became restless and in a hurry to reach the next checkpoint. My bum had become sore for whatever reason, and I was using a towel that I'd found along the way to ease the pain. After a long climb out of the saddle the towel had fallen off and I didn't want to go back after it, so I tried several things I came across like a piece of cardboard that I'd folded. Nothing worked. When I finally found a store in a town we passed through, I bought another towel. It helped, maybe, but the race had now become something I had to finish and no longer something I looked forward to doing. The change occurred without me knowing, much like it does in life. We go into things excited and with great plans, and somewhere along the way we get lost with all that is happening around us and forget the real reason we are where we are and can only focus on where we want to be next. My goal was to make Cap Rock Canyon by nightfall, but I was mentally spent and stopped in Turkey instead. I stayed in the old Turkey Hotel. It was old and run-down, really kind of eerie. After I checked in, Mark Pruett and Rick Presser arrived. We all had dinner together, along with a retired pilot who was staying there, it was nice just to talk to someone again. Only two days left, and I would have accomplished my goal!

Next morning, I headed off to Herford, the last checkpoint before Tucumcari. The day was pretty nice, but the miles ticked off so slowly. I felt like I would never finish and grew frustrated early. Then I formulated another plan. I could no longer think in terms of hundreds of miles to checkpoints; I had to break it down into small battles that kept my mind occupied. It became, *"Okay, only eight miles to Quitaque, and then only twenty-three miles to Post Office. Now, only 35 miles to Kress..."* and so on. Before I knew it, I was in Herford by nightfall. Life lesson: Set small goals to make the big goals much more attainable. I felt the need to go on to Tucumcari that night while the wind was low. No different than any twenty-four-hour race, it would hurt but was only 100 more miles. Dave called and said according to the View ranger apt, a navigational app used during the first Race Across Texas, all of us at the front were stopped in Herford, so I decided to get a good night's sleep and race tomorrow. The next morning, the other guys were smarter than I and left about four a.m. I didn't leave until six a.m. What a mistake. It turned out to be the toughest 100 miles I have ever ridden. The wind was furious at about thirty miles per hour, and there was not an object taller than a stick in any direction as far as one could see. At times, I found myself moving at a pace of about three miles per hour. Every time I stood to rest my back from leaning so far forward, my towel would blow off. I spent a good deal of time chasing that frickin' towel. Uphill into the wind, nothing could be worse except for the New Mexico Welcome Center, where I had planned on refueling, being on the opposite side of the interstate with huge fences between it and me. Worn out and tired, I simply again did what I do best—pressed on. By sunset I could see the lights of Tucumcari. What a beautiful sight! When I got to the finish line, Mark and Rick were there to welcome me. I had finished—and in fifth place at that.

Lying in bed that night it hit me like a ton of bricks: it was done! All the planning for months, the anticipation, the nerves, the not knowing what was to come, the adventure—it was over. Hate to say it, but it was emotional. I felt empty, not sure what I would do the next day. I then realized that the way I raced was much like the way I lived, in a rush. So many great memories of the last week came rushing back; even the hard times made me laugh. So many things, experiences, sights, and the beautiful awareness of being alive…I wished I could share it all with the ones I loved. If it were so great, however, why the rush? Why was I in such a hurry to get **from there to here? It reminded me of life, the way many of us live our lives. Always in a hurry to finish something, to get somewhere. Always complaining about the big picture album and never looking at the pictures. You know what I learned? I learned that where we come from not only makes us who we are but also that it's still there and should be visited from time to time to remind us of how we became who we are. I learned that it's easier to eat a cake one slice at a time, and that the taste lasts longer that way. I learned that to reach our destination we should sometimes drag our feet. God allowed us an adventure with a definite beginning and a definite end. The journey between those two points is what we make it. He thought enough of us to give it; the least we can do is take it and make it as great as we can.**

The house I lived in when I left home and the one I found myself
face to face with in the 2014 Race across Texas

Chapter 15

My Restless Soul Is Still Restless (The Stagecoach 400)

After finishing the 2014 RAT, I felt as though I was back in a prison. I was glad to be home, and I was happy to be back with family, especially Grandson. More and more, however, I felt something was still missing. There was still the need to be someone, to do something bigger and better. I already missed the race, and there were many days where I would find myself mentally back on the trail reliving the daily challenges. I was still yearning, but for what? I guess my soul was still restless, and perhaps it would always be. I read an article about a race out in California that was supposed to be a great warmup for the Tour Divide; some called it harder. Since it was only 400 miles, it seemed to be something I could do and not be gone a month. Four hundred miles would probably only take two days plus travel time; to and from the whole thing should be less than a week. After finishing the Race Across Texas, this would be simple. After all, I was now a seasoned veteran and wasn't worried about things not going as planned, so I signed up.

I had a Salsa Spearfish, carbon RS1, that I had just put together for a race that I hoped to do in the spring, the Arizona Trail 750. I outfitted it with the appropriate gear and rented a car. As usual, I worked right up to the race leaving myself two days to drive to California, set up my bike, and get a little food and rest before embarking on this journey. Waco to the starting point was only 1,400 miles, so I figured that should be more than enough time. After driving straight through, I arrived in Idyllwild the day before the race. That drive was a long one, but I was accustomed to doing things like that. I never was much on enjoying the scenery between points A and B. Oh, I had promised myself after the last race that I would enjoy the process, but surely that didn't mean stopping at every Buc-ee's, a truck stop, along the way. First things first, I needed to get my grandson a gift from California. I visited a couple gift shops in town and came across a stuffed puppy that I just knew he would love, and I got it for him. Little did I know that the puppy would become his childhood crutch. If you were to see Grandson, you would meet the puppy. I attended the racers' meeting later that night, and unlike the Race Across Texas meeting, this was just a bunch of people laughing and talking about their experiences in the race in previous years. I may have very well been the only newbie; I'm sure by my questions they all knew it. This time, however, I had a better understanding of what I needed to know before the race. This was less than half the distance of my last race, so I had settled on the fact that it was going to be a breeze, but I didn't want to take any chances. Most felt like the winner would do it in less than 2 days, which made me feel good because I knew I could do it in two days or just over that.

The roll out next morning was nice. The weather was what you would expect in southern California, blue skies and sunshine and just a bit chilly early in the morning, especially since Idyllwild is a small town that sits at the top of a mountain. I had a good game plan and was excited to begin. The race was simply a loop, down the mountain across the desert to San Diego then across some hilly desert terrain and back up another mountain ending where we started in Idyllwild. San Diego was only 200 miles and would be my day one resting place. Again, I had allowed my brain to mistake me for someone else. The race began with some awesome single-track that had a great flow to it. The scenery was simply beautiful—the trees, the trails, the wildlife—now, this was my kind of mountain bike race. Single-track, although fun, takes much longer to navigate than a gravel road. We were headed down the mountain, but I felt like most of my day was spent climbing. Tired from both the drive and the race, I stopped and camped at a place along the way with several other riders. Up early the next morning, I would spend the day making up for lost time, nothing but about 100 miles of desert and hills between me and San Diego where I would get a good meal and then move on towards Idyllwild. Well, news to those who haven't spent much time in the desert on a bike: it's hot, the sand is tough to ride in, and it's a slow process. Between 105 and 110 degrees all day, and in some places the sand was loose and thick it was like walking through quicksand. I remember reaching the wind caves late in the afternoon, and the shade they provided was much needed. As the night drew near, the temperatures plunged, and the sand got thicker. It became obvious I wouldn't make San Diego that day. As I exited the desert, I entered a small town and indulged myself at the local McDonald's. I tried to find a place to stay, but every place was full. I called my wife and told her how the day went and that I was a bit concerned about just sleeping by my bike up against some storefront. She got on the computer and found that I wasn't far away from a RV park. That was good news, and I holed up in an outdoor restroom at the park till morning. So much for finishing in two days.

The next morning things got much better, good roads to San Diego. The last twenty miles to the ferry that would transport my bike and me to the other side of the bay was windy, but it was better than 110 degrees in the desert. The ferry ride was great, and upon reaching land I found myself in the middle of an attraction area. People were everywhere, as were restaurants and gift shops. I remember thinking I had just gone from being alone on the moon to riding my bike in the zoo. After a good meal, I worked my way down the route through the hills and found myself on Highway 1 passing by Torrey Pines Country Club. It was hard to believe I had gone from sleeping in places like that to outdoor restrooms. I remember thinking, *"Man, there is a whole world out there that I know nothing about. People living so many different lives, and yet they, we, are only aware of ours."* Never in my wildest dreams did I think my concerns would go from what restaurant I would eat at after the round to where I could lie down and rest without getting killed. Life is truly a journey. I stopped by the ocean and took a few pictures and tried to keep a promise I'd made after the Race Across Texas to enjoy the journey.

I left San Diego and headed towards Idyllwild. The terrain quickly turned into rocky hills with patches of desert. It was getting late, and the sunset was beautiful. I had plans not to rest until I was through. As I began climbing just before dark, I spotted a big mountain lion upon a big rocky hill not fifty yards from the trail. It was beautiful, but honestly it made me a tad uncomfortable. After all, I was heading into the wilderness, and it was getting dark. As I pushed forward, I had this strange feeling I was being followed, but when I looked back no one was there. There were several places I had to walk. My legs were tired, and the grade was steep. I found a place to rest for a few minutes, and as I turned my bike around to stand it against a rock the light allowed me to catch a glimpse of something that terrified me. It was a mountain lion about thirty yards behind me, maybe not the same one I had seen earlier but a cat nonetheless. I didn't know if it was following me or just happened to be in the vicinity; either way, I didn't like it. I wanted to press on but didn't want to turn my back on this guy, so I got up against a rock and placed my bike in front of me. I then got out my pistol and just sat there hoping the cat would leave. I was tired and almost dosed off a couple times. I didn't want to leave my lights on for fear my battery would die, but I didn't want to lose sight of him either. After he disappeared, I was hesitant about moving on, but I did—stopping all too often to look at my surroundings. I spotted lights at the bottom of the hill and was so glad to see it was a convenience store. I knew I had to be getting close to civilization. I went inside to get something to eat and refill my bottles. There was a young lady working. It was about one in the morning, and so I jokingly said, "Where is everybody?" She smiled and said, "Not much traffic this time of the night." We made small talk, and I asked if I could just sit awhile to warm up and rest. She was so nice and invited me to put my bike behind the counter and said that I could rest in the storage room where I could turn off the lights. That sounded like a great idea, and I took her up on it. When I lay down, I fell right to sleep. Something awoke me, and I looked at my watch and couldn't believe it was about 3:30 a.m. I quickly got up, told the young lady how much I appreciated her hospitality, retrieved my bike from behind the counter, and headed back to the trail. It was cold, but the climbing soon warmed me up. At about 8:30 I arrived at the Hub Cyclery bike shop and signed the paper as being done. So much for a quick, easy ride—what an eye opener! I had breakfast and loaded my bike into the rental car and, yes, drove 1,400 miles nonstop back to Waco.

On the way home, I called everyone I could to help me stay awake and shared my experiences. While talking to my good friend, Coach Billeaud, he asked if I slept inside the church I had stayed at last night. I replied that I hadn't stayed at a church but spent some time resting in a convenience store. Tommy said, "Yeah, I watched you stop at the store, but then you rode four miles through a heavily wooded area to a church and stayed there till about 3:30 a.m. and then rode back to the store." I thought he had lost his mind. "Coach, I didn't go to a church. I slept in a storage room." He said, "Well, then, while you were asleep someone took your bike for a ride." Again, I brushed it off as him giving me a hard time. When I stopped to get gas, I pulled up the route on my Spot page, part of our new tracking system, and I couldn't believe what I saw. Somehow, my bike left the store, went through heavy woods to a church, and returned while I slept. Something was wrong, however; the trip took no time. The bike went there when I arrived at the store and left there when I left the store. Four miles in those conditions would have taken thirty minutes each way. My Garmin didn't show that segment, so I know I didn't ride there. When I looked at Google Earth, I saw that both the store and the church exist. The route is still posted to this day on Spot and still makes me wonder how. Maybe a glitch? Or maybe my soul just needed a safer place to rest. He is Lord.

My bike at the Pacific Ocean
during the Stage coach 400 in California

Chapter 16

The Tour Divide (God's Classroom)

The Tour Divide was like God's classroom. Looking back, I was a slow learner, but in the end, I got it. Everyday a new lesson, sometimes two. Lucky for me, God is patient. It was a journey like none I had ever experienced. I laughed, I cried, but mostly I was just quiet. The world around me was just quiet. It occurred to me I had been fighting a battle my whole life that I had no chance of winning. I had greatly underestimated my enemy. I had convinced myself that I could do anything, accomplish anything, overcome anything, and I could do so without any help. I needed only me. A war was fought on that long road from Canada to Mexico, and in the end, I lost every battle. And in doing so, I won the war. It would take a whole book to share with you all the things that took place during the race, and someday I may write it, but for now a short highlight reel will have to do.

After finishing the Race Across Texas, I was extremely excited about doing the Tour Divide. I started reading all the info I could that had been posted from those who had completed the route multiple times. Jay Petervary's list of equipment became my bible. I began the tedious process of buying the exact products that he used, many of which weren't easy to find. I packed and unpacked my bike till I could do it in my sleep. My thoughts were always on the segments that I had read about. Not a day went by that I didn't think about the Divide. I was ready, and 2015 was to be the year. Then the unthinkable happened. We sold our small ranch, which had been on the market for three years, and finding a place to live along with moving and finding land to build on suddenly took precedence over my race. I had many mixed emotions. On one hand I was so glad to finally rid ourselves of a place that was like a money pit, and I was looking forward to building the house of our dreams complete with an indoor bike shop. On the other hand, this would be the second time I would have to postpone the race of my dreams, and I wasn't getting any younger. The Race Across Texas was my Tour Divide in 2014 because my youngest Grandson was born on June 2 of that year and put a kink in my 2014 schedule. It was not a bad thing. I really wasn't as prepared as I thought in 2014, and that became evident with a measly 1,000-mile race across Texas in civilization with not much climbing at all. But this year I was ready, and disappointment, well, what I was feeling was much more than that. As I always say, "It is what it is," and 2016 would be the year. My second Race Across Texas would have to be my 2015 Tour Divide. I finished third!

Well, I finished my house and moved in late December 2015. I had a new Salsa Cutthroat on order, and my friend and mechanic, Matt Bates, and I had ordered everything we needed to build the perfect Divide machine. I had sold my Fargo and didn't have a gravel bike to train on, so I just rode my mountain bike on all my long training rides. Finally, in April, my bike came in and we got it built. I was a bit nervous getting such a late start on the build, fearing I wouldn't have enough time to work out all the kinks. My grandson's second birthday party was scheduled for June 2, and I had to be there. He had become my best friend, and even the thought of not seeing him for a month made me feel uncomfortable. It crossed my mind that again I might have to postpone the race. After all, it was just a bike ride, be it a long one, but a bike ride nonetheless. Then a series of events came about that made me realize I had to do the race. My wife at that time was teaching at a small private school, and one of her fellow teachers had a daughter, Emma Beth, the same age as my grandson. She was diagnosed with a malignant brain tumor, and after surgery she would need a full year of chemo. I couldn't imagine what I would do if that had happened to my grandson. At the same time, one of my good friends, Dr. Jim Olmstead, was diagnosed with stage 4 leukemia. Jim was the healthiest guy I knew and could ride as well as anyone a third his age. The world was telling me that life is short, and tomorrow, much less next year, is never guaranteed. If I were going to do the Divide, then I should do it now because the circumstances may never be what I need them to be for me to feel all is in order and can survive until I return. I decided I would race, and I would do it for Emma Beth. Maybe I could help raise funds for her and her family.

Many of my friends asked why I wanted to do such a thing as the Divide. They reminded me that it was dangerous and that I was old, both of which were true. As the date approached I thought about it, and it just made sense to me. Emma, a two-year-old, might not live to see age three. My mother-in-law, who never smoked a day in her life, died of lung cancer so young. A good friend lost his life in a fire just before he was able to retire. I watched one of my best friends wither away in a nursing home with me as his only visitor, although he'd spent his life helping thousands. Like most of us, I had seen tragedy strike without warning to so many who seemed so undeserving of it. I look around me every day and realize how blessed I am. Sometimes I question why. I certainly am not deserving of the life I've lived. I see so many who have so little and yet are happy. They don't blame the world for where they are; they just accept it and make the best of it. I remember thinking those who are so stricken with so many illnesses would trade with me and fight all the fears the Tour Divide offers in a heartbeat and with a smile. And if I could trade with them even but for a while, I would, but I can't. So I decided that my answer to those who asked would be, "I will ride because I can!"

I remember like it was yesterday saying goodbye to my grandson when I put him in his car seat after his party. He said, "Bye, Dandad, see you 'morrow." You see, we saw each other almost every day. I helped teach him to crawl, I taught him to take his first step and videoed it, I taught him to ride a bike early, and he spent hours riding with me and working on bikes in my bike room. He was a like a gift God sent knowing I was at a place in life where I needed a gift. Anyway, it was all I could do to make myself climb in the car that I had rented to drive to Banff. I convinced myself that I would be quick, and someday my grandson would be proud of his grandad for accomplishing such a feat. Dave, again a story for another time, drove me to Canada. That was quite the experience. I remember in Wyoming telling Dave that this must be the least inhabited place in the United States. Turns out I was right. It was a long drive, and when we finally reached Eureka Montana I felt as though we had crossed the US twice. We stopped at a storage shed I had rented and placed my small pistol in it, so I could retrieve it when I came back through. I couldn't take a gun into Canada, so this was a good place for it. The gun wasn't for bears or animals but more for the satisfaction of knowing that sleeping along the route by myself in the middle of nowhere might be a tad easier to do. When we crossed the border, the agent asked a few questions, and I was as honest as I could be. "Do you have any drugs in the car?" "Just prescription drugs, sir." "Do you have any weapons like a gun or bear spray?" "I do have bear spray, but I put my gun in a storage unit back in Eureka." "Pull over there, please, and get out of the car." Perhaps I should have skipped the gun answer. It took quite the explaining to assure the agents that I was a good guy, and after a search they allowed us to pass. As we reached Banff, Dave saw a bear on the side of the road and just had to stop and take pictures. I obviously wasn't interested and hoped that would be the last bear I saw except for in a zoo. My wife sent a video of my grandson in my bike room crying and screaming, "Dandad, where are you?" I'm not sure what she was thinking, but it took all I had not to turn that car around and go home. **I was beginning to realize that I was searching for things in life that I already had**. As Dave drove away, I started to think about how far we had come in an automobile with climate control and access to plenty of food and water, and it dawned on me what I was going to have to do on a bike twice that distance with none of the above. My initial thought was to catch that car, but then I got ahold of myself and realized I could use my phone to just call him and tell him to turn around. Why run? As fate would have it, AT&T and Canada were not getting along, and looking back I guess that's a good thing. I turned my attention to the task at hand and began to go over my plans, my bike, my gear, and the journey that awaited me.

The weather was beautiful the day before the race but was predicted to be much worse race day, and the prediction was right. A cold and overcast start was overshadowed by the festivities and Crazy Larry, who made us all laugh and momentarily forget about the obstacles that lay ahead of each of us. Finally, the moment of truth. We were off, and only 200,000 feet of climbing and about 3,000 miles lay between me and home. The journey had begun. Canada was simply beautiful beyond what I could have imagined. It was cold, and then it began to rain and sleet, but the surroundings had me in such awe I barely noticed. The woods were majestic, and other than a warning sign reading "bear in area," I loved all that the early part of the race had to offer. After about 60 miles we exited the woods to take a road that led to Bolton's Trading Post, the last place to get supplies for a while. I remember going downhill on a good road at about twenty-eight miles an hour and coming to a curve that made me think I should really slow down. I applied the brakes slightly at first then full, only to realize I had none. Panicked, I decided that laying the bike down was better than what was about to happen, and so I laid her down on the non-drive side like I had watched motorcycles do on tracks, only it didn't work the same way. My left crank arm and pedal caught the ground, and next thing I knew I was rolling over the bike and it over me. When the bike and I came to rest, I tried to hurriedly pick the bike up hoping no one saw my debacle and quickly realized my right hand wouldn't cooperate. I immediately knew from the looks of it that it was probably fractured. It was still frozen, so I didn't fully realize the extent of the injury until later that night. I walked the steep downhills and rode the rest until I reached the trading post. I tried to figure out the brakes, but in the rain and cold with no shelter I decided to wait until I could get someplace dry. I had planned on Sparwood for day one, but I was so slow I had to stop in Elkord for the night. Only a 110-mile day one, but I would easily get back on schedule once the brake situation was worked out. I was able to share a room with Hal Russell and several others at a motel, but I couldn't work on my brakes due to no light and because of my hand, so I decided to get some rest and fix them in the morning. Morning came, and my hand was purple and so swollen I couldn't get my glove on. Sparwood was only thirty miles, and the sun was out. My thinking was maybe Sparwood had a bike shop and could fix my brakes for me while I dealt with my hand. At the time, that was the longest thirty miles of my life. So much walking on the steep, technical downhills followed by hard climbs, not to mention hard trails to follow, caused me to take a whole day to get to Sparwood. I had plans to be in the United States by now, and I was frustrated to say the least. **Lesson 1: When we make plans, God just smiles**. When I got there, I got a room and started working on my brakes. The pads had frozen, and when I applied the brakes they were evidently pulled off the metal itself. I replaced them with a set of backup pads, which wasn't easy with my hand, and went down to get something to eat. I ate with a fellow rider I had seen a couple times that day on the trip, Lynn Estes. Later I walked to the market and got supplies for what was to be a long day back to the US. Sparwood to the border was only 120 miles, but it was through some of the most uninhabited country in North America, and it contained the largest population of grizzly bears in North America as well as "the Wall," a ridiculous hike-a-bike section of the trail. Regardless, it was "America or bust" for me. I was already a full day behind. I headed out early the next morning and spent most of that with Lynn. We were not riding together; we just couldn't separate. That wasn't all bad, especially since we were in the middle of grizzly bear country with no phone service. The trails reminded me of a movie, *The Good, the Bad, and the Ugly.* Some trails were simply riverbeds, some were awesome stretches of single-track, and others like the Wall bordered on ridiculous. The Wall was by far the hardest half mile I have ever climbed. I remember resting for a bit at Butts cabin and thinking, *"Wow, some made it to here on day one."* Lynn tried to convince me we should camp and get a fresh start in the morning, but I wanted to get to the US and get phone service even if that meant being by myself in this bear-infested wilderness, and so I continued. Soon Lynn was back with me deciding to continue as well. It was a long day. The last pass had snow and was cold and the descent into the border was steep and freezing, especially without a glove on my right hand since it still wouldn't fit. Finally, after about twenty hours on a bike, I saw a sign that read, "Welcome to the United States." The border agent asked me a few questions, and I replied with a simple no to each—lesson learned. There was a small camp area with a store that was gracious enough to sell me some leftover chicken strips and a 7 Up. Only ten miles to Eureka and the storage shed, so I decided to make it there and sleep for the night. As I started up the hill, it happened—my heart went out of rhythm. I took some extra meds, and since there was no way to stay on my bike, I pushed it for several miles. Finally, I found the shed and some much-needed rest. That was the first time since my last surgery at the Mayo Clinic that my heart had acted up, and mentally the fact that it could still happen after I was convinced that the last 13-hour surgery had fixed it, devastated me. I knew from past experiences I was entering a storm. Only three days, and my body was already beginning to break down. I was tired and somewhat deflated, and worst of all I was becoming a bit emotional. Three days, and already the thought that I might not make it was real.

The next day I got up late, and Lynn had already left. I guess it was about ten before I got out of the storage room, and I was trying to make up my mind whether I wanted to finish or just call it a day. The heart thing, the hand thing, it was already too much, and I missed my grandson dearly. Standing outside the storage facility I saw several bikes at a little restaurant, so I decided to go in. I sat and had breakfast with some fellow riders, and once they left I thought, *"Well, maybe I'll just give it another day. At least today I'll be riding with a group a little bit. I won't be alone, and I'm in the United States. If anything goes terribly wrong, perhaps I can get some help."* As I began to pedal I started feeling a little better. I'm not sure why, maybe I was a little less tense or too worn out to worry. Riding with the group didn't last long since most those guys were a bit faster than me, especially with my hand problem. Soon I found myself pretty much alone, but I was on the bike and moving nonetheless, and I felt so much better than I had the day before. I began to think perhaps this was not so bad. Maybe I could make it. It's funny how quickly the brain forgets and how quickly it can remember.

The first several days provided challenges that I had not begun to consider. Bears, hypothermia, fatigue, storms, treacherous trails, hunger, thirst, and the mind all are manageable when they exist alone, but as a group they become overwhelming. On one occasion, after a long day in the saddle, worrying mostly that my heart might get out of rhythm again, I decided to camp at the top of a mountain. Soaking wet at about 1:30 in the morning, I got my tent out and put it up while shivering violently. Then I took all my wet clothes off in the rain. I didn't want to put them in a one-man tent with me, so I laid them under the bike. I remember lying there mostly naked in my sleeping bag with just a hoodie and thinking how much I disliked the cold. Simply put, I was miserable. Outside, every noise I heard I imagined was a huge grizzly bear assessing how he was going to eat me and my tent. Finally, after about an hour, I decided my best bet was to get up and keep riding. I only thought I knew what miserable was as I stepped out of the tent into the rain, freezing rain. I had to put on those wet clothes that were muddy and lying on the ground soaked. Colder than ever, I tried to load my tent and everything back on my bike using mostly one hand, and what took maybe twenty minutes seemed like two hours. Extremely tired, anxious, and cold, my thinking turned to just getting down the mountain to a safer and warmer place. Heading down the mountain in the early morning hours, as I look back, wasn't one of the best ideas I ever had. Shivering so much that controlling my bike was a chore, and seeing a grizzly the size of an F350, I remember thinking, *"Dear Lord, if I get devoured by a bear, please make it quick and painless."* Morning couldn't come soon enough. **I wasn't beat; I was still riding. I did, however, settle upon a new rule: When it's cold and raining, you don't stop. You ride through it.**

Every day was virtually the same. I was on my bike, and I was going up an extremely steep hill. Mexico had to be the highest place on earth. It was a given I would wake up as tired as when I lay down, my bum would be sore, and the only variables were the sky and the temperature. Would it be sunshine or rain, cold or really cold? Arguments with myself became louder and lasted longer. Everything became an excuse to quit; no one would continue with a broken hand and a heart that was perhaps in no condition to be stressed this much. Mistake after mistake started to catch up with me; nothing I had spent years planning was right. It took much longer to cover the distances I had planned each day for a million unforeseen reasons. It seemed I was always arriving at my water and food refill spots after everything had closed causing me to have to camp early and wait for them to open the next day. Going to bed hungry was common, and frustration was like a headache that wouldn't go away. Finally, I had had enough. I couldn't fight anymore. There were a million reasons to just quit and not one reason to go forward. I'd fought against the world my whole life, and I never lost until now. I was tired, hungry, sore, depressed, and I missed my grandson and family. I had made up my mind that if I got to the top of another hill and could get phone service, I was going home. I thought for sure God would have helped me through this since I had a noble cause. Perhaps the cause was just an excuse to get the Lord on my side. I literally questioned every thought I had. The rain and cold weather was a thorn in my side as I climbed my last mountain, and then the skies cleared. My phone went crazy; I had reached the top and had phone service. Before I called,

I had to come up with the heroic version of why I was quitting. My family, that was my reason. How selfish of me, leaving them home to take care of everything while I chased some dream. I could get killed, and look where they would be. I would quit for my family. As I opened the phone, I couldn't believe the number of messages I had received. Before I dialed my wife, I made a huge mistake—I opened one. *Coach, we are so proud of you. We're following you on our phones and computers at work…Coach, I'm donating this much money for every mile you ride… Coach, I know it's hard, but Emma Beth can't quit fighting, so neither can you.* Be strong. If only I hadn't told people what I was doing I could end this suffering. What was I thinking? I want to go on, but I can't. I just can't. As I looked out over the mountains, the sky cleared to my left, and two rainbows appeared. They were so close that I felt like I was standing on top of them, and they extended as far down as I could see. I thought about the storms in my life and the rainbows that followed. Again, the world got quiet, and with tears in my eyes I put up my phone and began to pedal. My mind was quiet. No arguments, just an occasional whisper, *"A little farther, then I'll call."*

Water, something we all take for granted. Beginning in Canada through Montana and into Idaho there was plenty of it, and it was so clean most of the time I didn't even use a filter. Wyoming was a welcome site. It was warm and only had two states after it. I had finished Canada, Montana, and Idaho. Three down and three to go. It also meant that I would see the Great Basin up close and personal. It was beautiful in a weird kind of way. One could turn any direction, and there was nothing to see taller than a stick. Not much climbing and lots of sunshine— almost like heaven, yet it wasn't. My water turned so hot I couldn't stand to drink it, and I couldn't find the well listed as the only place to get water that was on our cue sheets. It's amazing how much energy you lose without water and how fast you lose it. It became obvious that I would die in the middle of nowhere from dehydration and asked God several times to spare me that fate. My prayers for water were answered as a storm full of thunder and lightning moved over me in a place that had no shelter within a hundred miles either direction. It remined me of the *Rhyme of the Ancient Mariner:* "Water, water everywhere and not a drop to drink." I was also reminded that one should be careful as to what one asks for. God has a sense of humor, of that I'm sure. I somehow survived the lack of water and the storm.

Colorado was much friendlier than the Basin, at least in the beginning. Brush Mountain Lodge was a cool place. Kristen is truly an angel, and my stay there is one I will remember always—pizza, beer, a nice fire, a warm bed, and time with good people. There was still a lot of climbing ahead. The sun was out. It was chilly, but temperatures were manageable, so all in all things were looking up. I stayed the night in Breckenridge, had a good meal, and set out early the next morning with the goal to make it to Sargents with a pitstop in Como and then Salida before climbing Marshall Pass and descending into Sargents. Just as I started the climb out of town the weather began to change, cold and lots of snow. The climb seemed to take longer than most, and as I finally reached the top, the sun broke through. Feeling good, I headed down the other side cold but glad to be going downhill, and with some speed. I had been climbing at about four miles per hour all morning. I looked down at my Garmin, and I didn't see a purple line. As I scrolled back it looked as though I had missed it by about four miles so. Back to climbing. I had not only missed the turn, but I was about three and a half miles from Como. A part of me wanted to just proceed, but I couldn't do it. I had followed every inch of the trail, no alternates, and I wasn't about to do it now. From Breckenridge to Como was only twenty miles, and it seemed as though I would never get there. After reaching the top of the climb, I had a hard time finding the Gold Dust Trail. That's where I needed to go. Finally, I spotted a delineator propped up by rocks and covered with snow. Wiping the snow back revealed I had found it, late but better than not at all. Besides, my wife always told me I had a bad habit of being late to everything. "You'll be late to your own funeral," she would always say, and on this journey I had proved her right thus far. Dropping into the Gold Rush Trail started out well and was awesome since I was a single-track kind of guy. It began to rain and get cold and muddy and most of all slow. Upon finally exiting the trail and entering Como, I was hungry, tired, and about four hours late. It was raining and cold and—you guessed it—no store, no nothing. I spotted an old man standing on a porch, and I asked about supplies. He informed me there was nothing and that even the post office only opened once a week for half a day. He must have sensed my frustration because he said he had an old place up the hill a bit that he and his wife lived in for fifty years that I could hole up in until the rain let up. He gave me some chips and water and led me up to the place. It was basically two old train cars connected on the sides, but it had an old wood burning stove and looked like a Hilton to me. I built a fire, dried my clothes over the stove, and watched it rain. It was peaceful, and I curled up on the floor by the fire and fell asleep. I awoke cold in the night and decided to just build the fire back up and wait till morning to head to Sergents. **It occurred to me that every hill I faced was always followed by a valley, and although my needs weren't always met the way I had hoped they would be, they were always met. I had all I needed and more. Every stop along the trail had allowed me to rid myself of some of the extra weight I had carried for far too long.**

Lynn and I crossed paths a lot, and quite frankly it was always good to see him. We were so opposite. I believed in Christ; he did not. I was a conservative and leaned right; he was a liberal and far left. Opposite but the same, two people fighting to finish what they had started. We were brought together for a reason, and of that I'm glad. After camping together one night near Sargents we both planned on making it to a campground just outside of LaGarita the next night. The next day the weather started out awesome, sunshine and blue skies, even a bit on the hot side. I had seen Lynn on an off all day. He was ahead of me, but occasionally I would catch a glimpse. As I passed a lake it seemed like a good place to stop and refill my bottles, so I did. Upon resuming my trek, I figured I had lost Lynn, but heck we were racing, and I decided I was going to reel him in. Settling in I rode hard for a good while, yet no sign of Lynn. I passed a guy headed the opposite way, and as we do along the Divide, I stopped and shook his hand. I asked if he had seen a guy up front, and he informed me that the rider was about ten miles forward. *"There's no way,"* I thought to myself. From that moment on, it was all out. Just as I started a climb, it began to rain, so I curled up by a stack of hay and ate what I had left in my bag. The rain and storm grew in intensity, and I decided it wasn't going to let up, so I headed up the pass anyway, Have I ever mentioned that I hate lightning? If not, I'm mentioning it now. It was so close I could almost touch it. I can't count the times I jumped off my bike and lay on the ground in the pouring rain thinking it might increase my odds of not getting hit. Lighting is nothing to mess with, and many people lose their lives every year hiking and biking. It seemed like the Divide brought every fear I had up close and personal every chance it got. Through it all, I somehow missed the campground and decided I could make it to LaGarita. Supposedly, there was a small store there where I could get supplies and dry out a bit. By now it was dark, and I was tired. I never found the store and was out of water, and the only option was to push on to Del Norte. I was sure Lynn probably had done the same. It appeared I could get there by maybe two or three in the morning, so a sidewalk outside a storefront would probably be my resting place. Tired and hungry, I began the climb up and over to Del Norte. It wasn't horrible, just frustrating. City lights would appear in the distance, and as I rode towards them, I would get a sense of relief—and then the trail would turn away. It was crazy. The trail down to town was treacherous and branched off constantly making it a challenge to follow the purple line on my Garmin. I came close to falling many times. Every time I had a bead on the city, the trail would turn away. The last turn away seemed to be for good, and I accepted the fact I now had missed three stops in a row and just needed to call it a night somewhere along the trail. Just as I rounded a corner, the trail came to a road. My Garmin said to go right, so I did. Half a mile later, I was in downtown Del Norte. I decided to call the number on the front door of the Old Windsor Hotel just for grins, and to my surprise a lady answered and came down to let me in. She had a room and allowed me to put my bike in the hall by the dining room. As I lay in the bed I thought about Lynn. I hoped he was all right and somewhere safe. I also wondered why I worried about so much that I had no control over. **I was beginning to understand that faith wasn't about everything turning out okay; faith was about being okay no matter how things turn out. As far back as I could remember, I had faith as well as trust—I had just placed them in the wrong person.** The next morning, as I was getting ready to head out, I got a text from Lynn. He had stopped at the Lake also, and somehow I had passed him. He said he spent the day trying to catch me, and upon reaching the campground he called it a day. Coming down the trail this morning to Del Norte, he had fallen and was hurt, so I decided to wait for his arrival. When he arrived, we had lunch together, and he contemplated calling it in. He decided to stay there for a day and recuperate, and I decided to do the same. The next segment was 14,000-plus feet of climbing and not much supplies for the next 174 miles—it wasn't a hard decision.

I was in New Mexico, the last state, and as with most journeys, the closer to the end the more difficult it becomes. The climbs were much shorter and much steeper, the weather was hot, the wind was in my face, the water was dirty, and I was tired. The finish line drew nearer, and my confidence began to increase. I was starting to trust in the right person, and the journey was beginning to feel comfortable. My surroundings became beautiful. Then I got a call from my wife. She was crying and felt I needed to quit and come home. She too was tired of trying to hold everything together while I played on my bike. If she had called a day earlier, I would have loaded up and gone home, but now I knew I had to finish. She was having a moment, and I knew she would be fine. I feel confident her breakdown was a test for me and that she was just the messenger. It reminded me of the Bible story of Jesus being tempted in the wilderness for forty days. I had an idea how he felt and appreciated the strength he gave me to carry on.

I was looking forward to reaching Pie Town and getting my piece of pie, a tradition for those on the Divide. As fate would have it, I reached Pie Town after everything had closed—my story since the beginning. It wasn't all bad though; at least I had a good place to stay. The Toaster House, given its name due to the hundreds of toasters all over it, was free to all Dividers. It was simply an old house that had mattresses on the floors and drinks, pizza, and chips in the kitchen. No one lived there, but donations made were used to leave supplies for those who passed through. It was perfectly placed to help one rest before the long trek to Silver City 184 miles away and 12,000 feet of climbing with nothing in between. The climb into Silver City was brutal, and the trail was impossible to follow. Lynn and I were together again and shared a meal and a room. I had decided the next day I would finish regardless of what the trail threw at me, and Lynn agreed to do the same. The next morning, we got an early start, and the trails were good. The day quickly became tough, though. It was hot, and the wind was in our faces the whole way. I kept telling myself it was only 124 miles to the border, and a sense of peace came over me. I knew I would finish. When we reached Hachita, Lynn was out of water and hot. Unfortunately, there were no services there. I saw a lady in a yard a street over and decided to ask her for water. Turns out, her husband had the keys to the little community room on the main street, and they had water there. When he let us in, he said that perhaps the old fridge would have some ice and we were welcome to it. The fridge had not only ice but bottled water and Jell-O. It was a true blessing, like an oasis in the middle of the desert. As we filled our bottles, I smiled at Lynn. Perhaps our conversations along the way about Christ were just me reassuring me, but so many times we were together, when things just worked out, I hoped perhaps somewhere inside Lynn maybe felt what I felt. Although it was just the two of us, we were always part of a bigger picture. **"Fear not, for I am with you; be not dismayed, for I am your God; I will strengthen you, I will help you, I will uphold you with my righteous right hand."** **Isiah 41:10**

We resumed our ride with a newfound vigor, and as we rolled up to that sign in Antelope Wells with watery eyes, we embraced each other, and for a moment two people with far different views had something in common: they had survived the toughest mountain bike race in the world, and no one could ever take that away from them. Lynn's parents were there to give him a ride, and a friend of mine, Don Baird, whom I had met in Leadville, offered to give me a ride. Don would arrive several hours later, so I sat quietly by the sign that read "Welcome to Antelope Wells" and reflected on the journey I had just completed. Overwhelmed with emotions, I cried, I laughed, and I gave praise to the Lord for taking time out of his schedule to ride 3,000 miles with me across the United States. He truly is Lord!

After the Tour Divide in 2016, I came to the realization that we as individuals are awesome and capable of so much more than we think. When faced with adversity, all too often we convince ourselves that quitting is the right thing to do. Quitting is never the right thing to do. There are multiple paths to success, but each path starts with you accepting that as truth. Yes, some ways are much easier than others, but the tough paths are usually the ones that we learn the most from and the ones that tend to shape who we are and who we are to become. Excuses are just part of the brain's way of helping us to avoid pain. Pain is simply weakness leaving the body. We must change our mindset to one that says we will succeed despite our perceived limitations, and that we all, though individually different in many ways, are born with all the tools we need. It's the mind not the body that determines our success. Did I want to quit? Yes, many times. Was there ever a good reason to quit? Yes, many times. But there was always a better reason to finish. The inner battles that we face will always be there, but right alongside them is the inner strength that also will always be there. Never be afraid to fail. Trying and failing is always better than accepting defeat without a fight. It's great to have a plan, it's great to have help, it's great to have unlimited resources, and it's even greater the moment you realize you have always possessed all three. Pursue whatever you do with a passion, be significant, and believe in yourself. There are many times when lesser athletes win the battle, a lot of David and Goliath stories, and it's okay to be David. Jesus Christ is Lord.

Two roads diverged in a wood, and I took the one less traveled by and that made all the difference, (*Robert Frost*)

The Tour Divide

Tour Divide

Listen my friends and you shall hear
A lone mountain bike in the granny gear.
You started in Banff seventeen strong
But this is a tale of things that go wrong

Achilles tendons and drifts of snow,
Grizzlies, big cats, nightmares-to-go.
Miles to go before you sleep
And all those promises to keep.

With lagging spirits and constant grief,
Utter exhaustion with no relief,
Wet, hungry, legs like concrete
Can't feel your toes, can't feel your feet.

Lugging your stuff, not to mention your bike
On this Rocky Mountain obstacle hike.
Some say that it was just never clear
They would need the skills of a mountaineer.

Swarming mosquitoes and one sore butt,
Mud everywhere, your wheels in a rut.
You've climbed 200,000 feet
And endured the desert's relentless heat.

Emotional ups, emotional downs
Mysterious maps, vanishing towns,
Swollen ankles, fever and chills
Slippery paths and a hundred spills

Awesome country these racers have seen -
Canada, Mexico and all parts between
from Banff in Alberta to Antelope Wells.
Each rider enduring their personal hells.

The prize isn't money, nor is it glory
It's just being part of an epic story.
It's you, your bike and your winning smiles.
You made it through nearly 3,000 miles.

It's meeting the challenges, seeing it through
Knowing the one who endured it was you.
Knowing you triumphed on this awesome ride -
Knowing you conquered the Tour Divide.

By Diana C. Gleasner Copyright 2008

The rainbows I saw when I went call home for a ride

Chapter 17

Race Across Texas 2018
(Still Restless
but with a Passion)

After returning from the Tour Divide, I felt better than I had ever felt in my life—and I don't mean just physically better but better in every aspect of the word better. Mentally I was refreshed; spiritually I was awakened; emotionally I was calm. I was asked to share my experiences with my classes at Baylor, with schools, churches, friends, etc., and I did so eagerly. My restless soul had finally found rest, or had it? As time passed, I found myself often somewhere along that trail in my mind, and the memories were so vivid and lifelike that at times I would get emotional. It was if I'd left a part of me out there, or perhaps it left a part of out there in me. Don't get me wrong, I was happy, and life felt better than ever before. I was enjoying so much time with Grandson who practically lived me us. We were putting the finishing touches on the house we'd built before I left. I started playing a little golf again and was enjoying it, and most of all, I was riding my bike with more confidence and pushing myself harder than ever. Life was good, yet not a day passed that I didn't relive some part of that race, but why? I'm not sure what was missing, but something was.

I decided to complete the Race Across Texas again later in the fall of 2016. All the thoughts of the daily struggles were now packed away somewhere in the back of my head, and all the good times were right up front and easy to get to. I was ready to race again, if only for seven days. After a good start in Texarkana, I started having butt problems, and at the end of day one, I had only traveled 191 miles. Day two got worse, and after forty miles I called my wife to come get me. This was new to me; I had never quit any race before. Maybe my butt was still not totally recovered from the Divide. In early spring I tried my hand at Billy Rice's St. Joe's 500-mile Grand Fondo. Robert Parish, one of my students, decided he'd like to go with me. It sounded like a lot of fun; after all, Robert was one of my favorite students and a strong rider. He built up a bike and said he would catch me somewhere along the trail and ride with me. He caught me at about mile 80 and road another 110 miles with me before we decided to camp. The next day my knee was shot, and again my wife came to my rescue. Two fails in a row: what extremely bad luck. Robert and I paired up again to do an ITT from Tucumcari, New Mexico, to Texarkana, Arkansas, later that summer.

We chose to do a west-to-east route, and we were off to Tucumcari. The first couple days brought a bit of trouble in the form of rain and mud, which resulted in a sloppy mess. That was followed by an onslaught of flats, which was followed by more torrential downpours and wind. After about 600 miles, Robert informed me that there was something wrong with me for doing these kinds of things. He had a point, and we had Dave pick us up. I thought 600 miles for Robert was awesome, and I've always known something was wrong with me. Three attempts to race since the Divide and three fails. I began to think that the Tour Divide had taken everything I had and that I couldn't race anymore. This ate at the very core of my existence. What was going on, and how could I fix it?

I felt I had to break this curse, and so I decided I would be the first to ride a single-speed from west to east across Texas—1,029 miles, a lofty goal. As I begin the process of building a new bike for the challenge, I felt the need to make some changes. I chose a steel frame from Spot Brand bikes because of the Gates belt drive and how well it worked with the bike itself. A Lauf fork to tame some of the washboard, a new K-lite for reliability, a couple Chafe bags from Bike Bag Dude to keep my water cooler, and a Bar Yack for a little comfort with a small sticker placed on it that I read daily: "**With men this is impossible, but with God all things are possible.**" I carried a minimal amount of supplies because it was Texas not the Rockies, and it was hot. I finished the bike by placing a Brooks B-12 saddle on it, a suggestion by Hal Russell. As the dates I set approached, things begin to get a bit stormy. The rental car wasn't what it was supposed to be. I had a ton of lessons and not as much time to pack as I would have liked and more.

Importantly, I was tired, and my heart was a bit out of rhythm all week. Cheryl asked me not to go, but I felt I needed to. I had to prove I could finish one of these things. After all, I had completed the 3,000-mile Tour Divide. This was something I should be able to do, and I needed to do it. Cheryl drove me to Tucumcari, and we arrived late in the afternoon. We got a room at the Roadrunner, a great place, and I unpacked my stuff and prepared it for the next day. Then we walked across the street and grabbed a bite to eat. By the time we got back to the room, I was dizzy and feeling horrible. I set my alarm for 4:00 a.m. and told Cheryl I was probably not going to be able to go—I'd get up, however, and decide then. I didn't sleep much that night, and four came early. I told Cheryl I was going to give it a go. I told her to sleep in and try to call me before she left in case…well, in case this was to be fail number 4.

As I left Tucumcari headed to San Jon, the wind became brutal and was dead into and at about twenty-five miles per hour. I had a bit of a reprieve as I turned towards the Cap Rock, but then back into it again, and the heat was ridiculous—104 to 110 degrees all day. I made it to Russell's Travel Center and was beginning to feel better. Cheryl called and asked how I was doing, and I told her I was better, just not 100%. She decided to go to Vega, where I planned to stop for the first night, and check on me. It was so hot that I welcomed the wind. My water stored in my Bike Bag Dude bags stayed drinkable, but my other bottles were just too hot to drink. To cool off, I once jumped in a cattle trough full of algae and was okay with it. The first three days were brutal— the canyon, the red roads—they all earned their reputations. The good thing was that I was starting to feel better, and I hadn't noticed my heart in a while. The fourth day was an eye-opener, to say the least. Coming into Henrietta, the roads were good, and it was Father's Day, which gave me a lot to think about. There is about a four-mile stretch where the only way to get back to good gravel roads is to cross the Dam and ride through the lake park facilities on a paved road. As I crossed the Dam, I stopped and took a few pics. It was later in the afternoon, and the evening was much cooler and less windy. Getting back on my bike, I begin my trek with the thought of getting back to a shoulder and off the dam. I heard what sounded like a car racing ahead of me, and when the car came in view around the corner I remember thinking, *"Who drives that fast in a park, and especially going around a curve?"* As we grew closer together, a weak feeling formed in my stomach. He was going too fast to make the turn, and in an instant, I was airborne. Things seemed to move so slowly, and as I lay on the ground I realized I had been hit head-on by a car. People were telling me all kinds of things, none of which registered. All I could think about was that I need to get up and get back on my bike; this couldn't be real. The person who had hit me drove away and just left me there. Once I could stand, I only cared about my bike. I couldn't believe it, but it was ridable. "I must go," I told the officers, "And no ambulance. I need to finish this race." It took a good bit of convincing, but they let me leave. I had cuts, and my helmet was broken, but I felt okay. My phone wouldn't work except for texting, and I kept thinking how I would have called for help if no one had been there. An extremely nice family followed me close behind with flashers until I made my way to the gravel again. I told them thanks, and before I could head out, another cop stopped me with another battery of questions. I said I was fine, to which he replied, "If you were fine, you would know better than to head down the road you're about to go down." I asked why he felt that way, and he explained it was full of rattlesnakes, wolves, and wild boars, and it was dark. I replied, "If there are no cars, I'll be fine." As I found myself back in the woods, a calm came over me. I knew I should have died on that bridge, but I didn't. God still had plans for me or I would've—that's the only explanation. The gravel emptied me into a hotel parking lot in Henrietta. I asked the lady if she had a room of any kind; I just needed rest and to call my wife. Her face, as well as the faces of those in the lobby, said it all. "Are you okay?" she asked. I replied with a very polite, "Yes ma'am." "You look like you have been hit by a car," she said. I could not believe that it had happened; it had to be a dream. As I looked down and I saw myself for the first time, I was stunned. I really had been hit by a car. When she saw the look on my face, she asked in an almost panicked voice if I needed a doctor. I said, "No, ma'am, just a bed. I'm going to rest awhile and get back on my bike and finish this race." Another lady standing in line asked, "Are you married?" I thought that was strange, but I replied, "Yes, ma'am." She asked if my wife knew, and I said no, but I was about to call her. "If you want to finish your race, you might want to skip that call. 'Cause I know my husband would be done. There would be no more biking."

They got me a room, and after I wrapped my head around what had happened I was even more determined to finish what I had started. I convinced myself that if God had wanted me, I wouldn't be in this room preparing to make the worst phone call ever. My wife had just texted me earlier that day about a hit-and-run that killed a man just down the street from our house. In the last year, I had lost four friends to hit-and-run drivers and a couple more in Waco that I didn't know. My saving grace with her was that I am rarely on roads. This call, however, was not going to go over well. I used the hotel phone to call her, and she immediately asked what was wrong. I told her it had been a long day and made some small talk about the house and pets and my grandson. She again asked what was wrong, and I said, "Cheryl, I am all right" and she started crying and asked what had happened. When I told her I was hit head-on by a car doing about sixty miles per hour, she fell apart. "You come home now. We need you, your grandson needs you, please come home." It was a hard conversation, but I convinced her that God is good all the time and that I needed to finish. After we hung up, I lay on the bed and fell asleep exactly like I was. I slept about three hours, and then I was up and back on my bike—quite sore, I might add, but on my bike nonetheless.

I rode hard the next couple days on the bike, seventeen to twenty hours a day. I was sore—my shoulder and my back hurt—but I rode. When I reached Paris, I rested for the final push the next day. It was about 3:00 a.m. when I got there, and I left at 7:00 a.m. I had seen Kevin in Oklahoma; he was one of several who were following my progress online and took the time to come out and support me. When I left Paris in a mist that last day, a local gentleman rode through town with me like I was a hero. The support made me feel better and gave me more reason to push forward. The weather turned horrible, severe thunderstorms full of lightning. The trail became a muddy mess. I grabbed shelter in a garage during a severe portion of the storm at a house where no one was home. When it let up, I got back out there and somehow made a wrong turn and wound up at the same house ten miles later. It was already a 180-mile day without all the extras. Sometimes I felt there was a force trying to stop me from finishing, and that it had been with me all week. Gary Tucek and the Avery Fire Department offered me a place to stay with about sixty miles to go, but I just couldn't do it. I had to finish. When I got to New Boston, the rain had let up, and I only had forty miles to go. This was about midnight. I stopped at a store I passed to get a chocolate milk, and my wife showed up. She was going to pick me up earlier in Texarkana and take me home after I finished, only the storm had put me behind. She found me by following me online. "You should rest and finish tomorrow," she said. But I said, "No, I want to break eight days. I must ride." The roads were mostly wet gravel roads covered by snakes and frogs. Many were tree-covered and dark but extremely quiet except for the occasional dog that wanted a piece of me. I rode at a pace of about ten miles per hour. I just couldn't get much more than that out of my single-speed at the time. Cheryl followed me for four hours to the chamber building where the race officially ends. After she picked me up, we found a hotel, and I showered and then lay down. I knew when I took off my clothes that I was in trouble. I had bruises the size of volleyballs all over me.

Know what though? I rested with a peace in my heart. I knew that no matter what the world threw at me, I could handle it as long as I had God with me. I felt as though this race was a gift to remind me of His support and protection. **Not my fourth fail in a row but my first win, understanding that all is out of my control, and that's a good thing.** As far as getting hit by a car, well at least it won't be by the same guy. They caught that young man—no insurance, not his car, and his fourth DWI. I pray that his storm leads him to a place where he realizes he's not alone. Many times in my life, had it not been for the grace of God, I could have very well found myself in his shoes. I have several surgeries scheduled this fall from the accident. While mending I'll be mentally preparing for a race I'm doing in the spring. Race Across Texas 2019 to "there and back", a YO-YO. In other words, from Texarkana to Tucumcari and back without stopping. I have no doubt it will be an adventure with many "I wasn't expecting that!" moments. I also have no doubt that God will make the trek with me and that my education will continue.

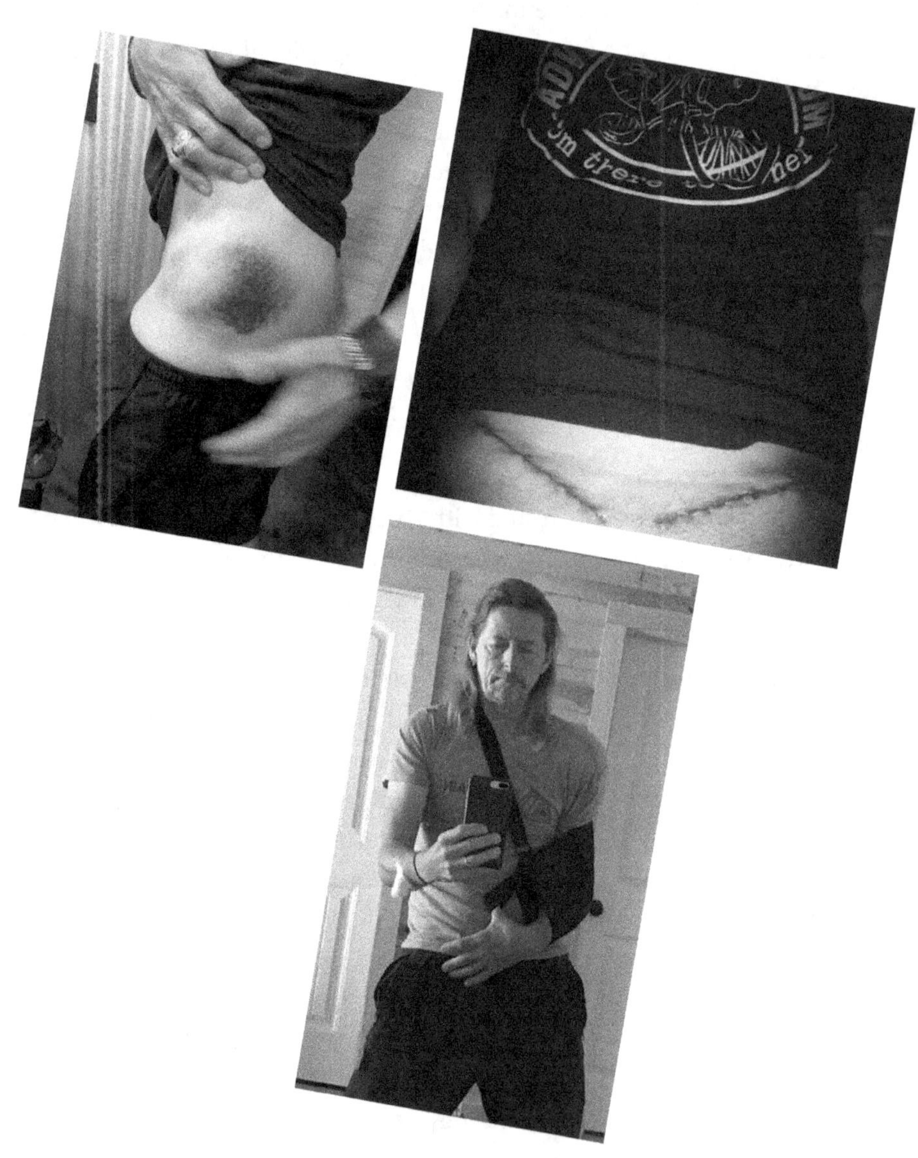

Right after I got hit by a car during my 2018 Race across Texas

Chapter 18

Thankful for the Journey

I am now convinced that there is no rest for a restless soul, and that's okay. What's important is how you deal with it. We are restless because something is missing in our lives. That something, I'm convinced, is Christ. I need to ride because it allows me to spend time alone away from the world with only the Lord to talk to and depend on, and that is good for my soul. The world fills all our lives with so much excess weight that there is little room for Christ. For me, the longer I ride, the more I rid myself of that weight. "Every ounce counts," as my good friend Matt Bates would always say. Only carry what you need. For me, Christ is my rock, my fortress in whom I take refuge. I remember reading a passage in the Bible that always bothered me. It makes much more sense now.

> *1 John 2:15-17: [15]Do not love the world or anything in the world. If anyone loves the world, love for the Father is not in them. [16]For everything in the world—the lust of the flesh, the lust of the eyes, and the pride of life—comes not from the Father but from the world. [17]The world and its desires pass away, but whoever does the will of God lives forever.*

That verse always bothered me to some degree because I loved everything about the world—its beauty, its difficulties, passion, emotions—everything about life is so awesome. Or is it? You see, when your eyes have been opened and your heart has been healed, you realize the world is not what it seems. It's a place filled with distractions, with things that make you forget what's important. Some are disguised quite well like love, happiness, and wealth. Others are in your face like death and destruction. We pride ourselves on our accomplishments as if we were the only ones responsible for them. We blame our failures on others, and no matter how we spin it, the truth is it's always about us.

As I look back on my life, I am so thankful for the journey. The ups and downs, the good and the bad, the triumphs and the failures, all of which make me who I am, and none of which I would trade for the world. If I were to lay down tonight and close my eyes never to open them again, I would want the world to know how thankful I am for the life God so graciously blessed me with, a far better life than I deserved. I believe in free will and that regardless of our trailhead or our destination, we choose the path we ride. I also believe God is there beside us every turn of the cranks. Like a child, we often choose not to listen to His advice. We ride too fast through areas we should walk, and we all suffer the consequences of those actions. I am just thankful that He allowed me to fall but was always there to pick me up, that He opened my eyes when I chose to keep them shut, that He provided a light when all around me was dark, that He replaced my anger with love, that He cared for me when I did not care for myself, and most of all I am thankful that He answered every time I called His name. In the movie *The Book of Eli*, Denzel Washington said a prayer at the end that has always stuck with me. I mention this because I include several parts of the prayer in my prayer each day.

Dear Lord, thank you for my life and thank you for helping get this far. Thank you for the good I've done, and I am so sorry for the bad. In the days I have left on this earth I ask that I may do more of the first and less of the second. I thank you, Lord, for the storms, for without them a rainbow would have no meaning. Thank you for keeping me resolute when all around me seemed lost. Thank you for the angels you filled my life with that helped me to find a path when there was none. Thank you for my grandson and the change he made in my life, and most of all, Lord, thank you for Your Son and the sacrifice He made for me. Forgive me, Lord, for being a little tired. It's been a long day on the bike, but I will keep the faith. I will continue to fight the good fight, and, Lord, I will finish the race. Amen

Chapter 19

Angels along the Way

s I look back through my life, there are so many people that I am thankful for and each of whom I met at the exact time I needed to. Angels, I would say, placed along my path at times when God knew I would need them. A lot of my nonbeliever friends will say they were coincidences; just like life and the universe, they have no meaning. And to them I would say this: The fact that there had to be literally tens of trillions of coincidences happen at the exact right time for creation of anything to happen is in itself a miracle. Where there is a creation, there must be a creator. Every living thing has unique characteristics, and everything about their existence is orderly. Nothing is random. *Proverbs 8:17: I love those that love me, and those who seek me shall find me.* We can exist in life justifying things in a way that fits our needs, but in death we will be naked as we were in birth, and our final resting place will be determined not by how we lived our lives but rather if we were smart enough to understand our shortcomings and accept a gift from Someone who loved us before we came to be. **There are two things I know to be true: death is a certainty, and God is real.**

> **Exodus 23:20** "See, I am sending an angel ahead of you to guard you along the way and to bring you to the place I have prepared.

> **Psalm 91:11** For he will command his **angels** concerning you to guard you in all your ways;

Uncle Ray and Aunt Connie were placed in my life when I was a young boy who had just moved out on his own and had no one to help him. I didn't know them very well, yet they served as my parents when I had none. They fed me and prayed for me and supported me through all the mistakes I found myself making on a regular basis. They co-signed for me to get cars, Uncle Ray took a huge chance and got me a job with the company he worked for, and they were the only family I had present at my wedding. I would have never made it in life if they had not of been there. They were the second set of angles sent to help guide me. My great-grandmother was the first.

Cheryl Lamb, my wife. I guess the person I talk about the least is the one who has helped me the most. I'll never understand what she saw in me the first time we meet, or why she has put up with me my whole life. She was the one who took me from where I was to where I am. She stood by me in every sense of the word. She took a backseat to everything I did, yet she encouraged me without fail. Cheryl is the person she admired most; she is her mother in every sense of the meaning. The best mom our kids could have ever hoped for and a way better wife than I ever deserved. There's no doubt that I have suffered from the mistakes I made, but she suffered from them more. To this day, she does without until she feels everyone has all they need—and she never feels everyone has all they need. She has always been about family although she has never been blessed with one like she had always dreamed of. I know God will make it right on the other side. I just hope someday she will smile the way she did when I met her. She's not just a beautiful woman with a beautiful soul; she is and has always been the rock in my life. Without her, I would have never made it from there to here.

Bob and Bonnie, my wife's parents. I can't begin to understand the sacrifices they made for me. Allowing their daughter to marry a guy with as much baggage as I had is something I am eternally grateful for. Bonnie treated me like a son from day one. She was the best Christian I ever met and loved the Lord with all her heart and soul. I miss seeing her play the organ at church every Sunday, hearing her laugh, and most of all, making my wife smile. Bob encouraged me to get a GED and go back to school. He convinced me I could do better, be better, and have a life better than I had ever imagined. They both supported me when I let their daughter down and never gave up on me, unwilling to push me aside. They held fast to their beliefs. I was not just the man their daughter married; I was family, and family never gives up on family.

Mac Hickerson, the definition of an angel. A man who gave me a reason to go to school by allowing me to be a part of the University of Mary Hardin Baylor golf team. Without golf I would have never finished school, and somehow, I think Mac knew that. Mac took me under his wing and taught me more about how to be a man than anyone before him. He taught me how to accept responsibility for my actions, how to accept both success and failure, and do it with an attitude becoming of a man who understood there was more to life than winning and losing. He took us, the team, and our families and made us a part of his family. We shared Christmas together, we laughed about his swing, and we cried as he and I watched the shuttle explode together at his desk. I have called him to share my successes, and I've called to admit my shortcomings. In each case, his words were always kind and spoken with heartfelt meaning. Mac was my college coach, my mentor, and most of all, Mac is my friend. I am forever thankful that God placed him in my path.

Joel Williamson, my college teammate. It would take a whole book to explain mine and Joel's relationship. He has been a friend since college, a partner in countless tournaments and businesses, and someone I've been with through some good times and some bad. It's funny the role certain people play in your life that you never saw coming. I never dreamed that, as I watched Joel curl up in the fetal position after four-putting from three feet, that years later he would be my caregiver as I lay in bed struggling to breathe in the Mayo Clinic in Minnesota. People brag about how many friends they have on Facebook and social media. As for me, I have fewer friends than I have fingers on one hand. I'm thankful to say he is and always will be one. That being said, I'm still somewhat upset about that four-putt.

Another person who played a huge role was Charles Norris, Old Charlie, as everybody called him. Charlie and I became friends at Bob Ammon's driving range. Charlie was a special person. He had been a senator in Oklahoma, was declared a prince of the Chickasaw Nation and renamed Oklahoma A&M to Oklahoma State University. He became a dear friend and a father figure to me. He worked for me for several years and never took a penny, and he let me know about it frequently. He had sold his business and beautiful home in Dallas so that he and his wife could move into a small house on Alexander to take care of his bedridden mother-in-law. His wife, who was a registered nurse, unfortunately passed away and left him to take care of his mother- in-law until she passed. He gave up a life of leisure to be there for his family and never once complained. From a senator to a guy picking up balls by hand every night out of a field for no pay. Charlie will always hold a special place in my heart. He later passed away in a nursing home with my wife and me, and occasionally Bob Ammon, as his only visitors. I saw him three times a week for as long as he was there. I kissed him on the forehead one Tuesday night and told him I loved him and that he had fought the good fight and that it was okay to rest. He passed away the next morning. His service was me speaking to about five people. A man who served his country both as a veteran and a senator, a man who helped thousands of people and never asked for anything in return, left the world with an old bag of clubs, which contained his trash can pitching wedge, and a couple pictures on the wall, all of which reside in my shop to this day. Charlie was my friend from Tishomingo, Oklahoma, to whom I owe 126 Dr. Peppers due to many late-night chipping contests that I still protest.

Jordan Cox was placed in my path for two reasons: to help me understand that I am not the teacher I thought I was, as evidenced by his inability to chip a golf ball successfully, and to help me grow spiritually. I have learned so much about the Bible from Jordan. He has spent hours on the phone walking me through so many difficulties and used the Bible to answer so many questions. He has always been there for me and willing to help me find the truth and has done so with patience and kindness. His trust in and walk with the Lord has been one I have not only respected but at times even envied. Our many conversations about Christ helped guide me to where I am today and, more importantly, helped guide me to where I will spend eternity. Jordan has touched the lives of so many, and I am fortunate to have been one. *And I heard the voice of the Lord saying, "Whom shall I send, and who will go for us?" Then I said, "Here am I! Send me."*

Jon Antunes came into my life when I was tired. I needed to hand off the baton, and I couldn't have asked for a better answer to a prayer. He is a dedicated father and husband, a great son, a good friend, and most importantly, a man who loves the Lord. Just another blessing God chose to share with me.

Fred Schmid, a friend whom I have a lot of respect for. If I had a choice to ride with anyone who ever rode a bike day in and day out, it would be my grandson, and a close second would be Fred. He is and always will be my biking hero. I'm sure I have enjoyed our time together much more than he has; he was usually the one waiting on me. The thing is, he was always willing to wait and has always treated me as an equal when I am far from it. He is my Arnold Palmer and a big reason why I fell in love with this sport. He may feel differently now, but I have no doubt someday we will enjoy suffering on a bike together on some old backroad in a place far greater than the one we ride in now.

From time to time God still reminds me of where I've been and how I got to where I am, and for that I am thankful. A young lady in my class was one of those reminders. One of the biggest storms I faced was the heart problems I had beginning in 2008. In the fall of 2014 I witnessed firsthand how God uses us to do his work, and I saw the rainbow clearly for the first time in my life. A girl in my mountain bike class started crying during our ride one day while we were climbing a hill. All the other students were well ahead of us. I got off my bike and put my arm around her and asked if she was okay, and she replied that she was scared. I hugged her and said, "Don't be scared, girl. You don't have to do anything that scares you. This class is about having fun." She said, "No, that's not it; it's my heart." I almost passed out, I was so taken, when she said, "I've had three heart surgeries, and I'm scared!" I asked her if she had gotten permission to take the class, and she said, "Yes, but when my chest tightens I get scared." Here's what I told her:

> Molly, I'm glad you are taking my class. Thanks for sharing your situation with me. I totally understand how you feel and have those same feelings from time to time myself. After my last surgery, I really felt horrible for quite some time. I had always been so active, and out of nowhere, all of a sudden, I had had three heart surgeries and still wasn't fixed. My doctors assured me that I could resume most of my normal activities, and that if the symptoms got worse in a few years we would try another surgery since advances were being made almost daily. I started out being so cautious because I was afraid. I would cause the problem to resurface. Every time my heart got out of rhythm, I panicked. I spent months being afraid,

and then one day I realized I was still here and that when God was ready to take me, He would, regardless of how healthy or unhealthy I might be. I never push my religion on anyone, and I am by no means pushing it on you. I feel I am still here because God still has plans for me. I took up cycling after my last heart surgery and made myself look past the fear and continue to live my life. I have pushed myself beyond the boundaries that a **stupid disease tried to set for me**. I race twenty-four-hour mountain bike races that physically drain me to a point I can't even begin to explain. I am racing a 2,781-mile race through the wilderness this June from Banff, Canada, to Mexico unsupported—pretty cool. Will my heart get out of rhythm at some point in time while I'm alone in the middle of nowhere? Probably, but I will push on because I know I am blessed to be alive every day, and I will enjoy every minute that I am here.

I am not suggesting that you push yourself beyond what the doctors tell you is safe; that is something you should never do. I am simply saying I understand where you are, and being scared is normal. I hope, however, that you push past that fear and realize as I did that you are here because God still has plans for you. I don't believe God gives us the problems we have—those we inherited from an imperfect world—but I do believe he can use those problems to accomplish much good and His will. We will have a fun semester, and anytime you want to talk, just let me know. Hope I am not out of line with this; I just want you to know that I care and that I will do all I can to make this class as enjoyable as possible for you. Anytime you need to rest or want to skip certain activities, that will be all right with me. Do only what you feel you are comfortable with, and that will always be enough.

Here is the email she sent me after class:

Thank you so much for taking the time to listen to me today and share your story too. I have a hard time explaining myself, even to my doctors, because they don't know what it really feels like to have a heart condition. I am very thankful to be able to hear how you have overcome your heart problems even though they aren't entirely fixed. I've had my condition my whole life and just now starting to be afraid because of it. It is hard for me to tell if there is a real problem or if I just need to push through the pain to have a stronger heart. I really don't want my heart condition to stop me from trying new things or doing things I enjoy. Even more, I am thankful of your testimony of what God has done in your life. It's crazy, but knowing God, it's not so crazy that the day before your class I passed out after exercising. God knew that you would be faithful in sharing what He has done in your life during a time when I really needed someone to tell me to keep fighting. Someone that can actually relate to how I might be feeling. I probably won't be the best mountain biker by the end of the semester, but my hope is to trust God a little more each time I ride and to let Him take away that fear.

Thanks again for your support. I'll see you soon, Molly

God not only used me to help Molly, but God used Molly to help me. God chose Molly to remind me of some things that I tend to forget. It's easy for me to forget about what's important when things are going well, and I tend to only seek God's help when things are not great. I had almost forgotten about how difficult my health problems had been and more importantly how God got me through them as well as so many other tough times. Molly helped me remember. :)

Storms have a purpose; embrace them and trust a rainbow will follow.

"God doesn't call the qualified;
God qualifies the called."

9 798765 740699